eDs

By Kera Bolonik

The Official Companion Book to the Hit Showtime Series

SIMON SPOTLIGHT ENTERTAINMENT

New York   London   Toronto   Sydney

SIMON SPOTLIGHT ENTERTAINMENT

An imprint of Simon & Schuster

1230 Avenue of the Americas, New York, New York 10020

© 2007 by Lions Gate Television, Inc. All Rights Reserved.

All rights reserved, including the right of reproduction in whole or in part in any form.

SIMON SPOTLIGHT ENTERTAINMENT and related logo are trademarks of Simon & Schuster, Inc.

Designed by Jane Archer and Margaret Gallagher

Manufactured in the United States of America

First Edition 10 9 8 7 6 5 4 3 2 1

Library of Congress Control Number 2007925443

ISBN-13: 978-1-4169-3878-1

ISBN-10: 1-4169-3878-8

CONTENTS

Welcome to Nancy Botwin's Neighborhood

An Introduction to *In the Weeds*

The first time I watched *Weeds*, I thought it was the most heartrending series I'd ever seen. I was a latecomer, so I had the good fortune to take season one in a single, mind-altering hit, thanks to a set of review-copy DVDs. What particularly resonated with me at the time was its raw depiction of grief experienced not only by the Botwins, who were each coming to terms with the loss of Judah in his or her own way, but also by Celia Hodes, who was mourning a life of disappointment and unfulfilled expectations, whether or not she was aware of it. The next time I watched *Weeds*, I thought it was the funniest show I'd ever seen, and for

many of the same reasons . . . not to mention the debates on "runways" versus "taints," city council election campaigns, lectures on masturbation, health-conscious gangstas, and pit bulls with necklaces and an appetite for toes. *Weeds* is both heartrending and funny, a "dramedy" in the truest sense, and as such it is the boldest, most innovative series on television—because it dares to follow an emotionally charged moment with a laugh-out-loud hilarious exchange, sometimes within the same scene. It's a lot like life in that way.

"We're sincerely going for a combination of pathos and comedy and I don't think the two are mutually exclusive," says Robert Greenblatt, president of programming at Showtime Networks, Inc. "It's only called a comedy because it has comedic moments, so it falls on the comedy side of the equation, but usually comedy is a very reductive label."

Executive Producer Jenji Kohan has created a series with characters and themes as substantive, lyrical, and profound as any great novel. Missing an episode has the same impact as skipping a chapter of a book. *Weeds* was not the first series to have this quality—this television convention was largely born with *The Sopranos* in 1999. But it was clear from the moment it premiered on August 7, 2005, that *Weeds* would take this kind of televised storytelling to a whole new level, with characters we may recognize from our own lives—some of them, like Celia or Andy, who lend voice to our most embarrassing or unpleasant thoughts—and gritty, bold dialogue that mirrors the way we really talk to each other. In thirty-minute helpings, this iconoclastic show at once cleverly explodes the myths about American suburbia by yanking back the curtains on three very different families, all of whom are struggling to survive their respective predicaments. "It's the truth, and the truth isn't always comfortable and it doesn't always flatter you," says Co–Executive Producer Roberto Benabib. "That's kind of the hallmark of the show."

Nancy loves her boys, but to her, "dealing" means selling drugs. A danger junkie, Nancy is fearless in the face of gangster thugs with automatic weapons, but terrified of confronting her sons about their feelings in the wake of their father's death. Her brother-in-law, Andy, is an attentive surrogate parent, but his judgment is usually impaired by his philosophy that most problems can be solved with a simple tug of the tiger.

Nancy's Agrestic neighbor Celia Hodes rails against drugs, sex, and overeating, while popping Ambien, diet pills, and an old quaalude; swilling martinis; and cheating on her husband not once, but twice. Her daughters hate her for scouring their diaries and using nanny-cams to expose them, and her husband lives in fear of her. Heylia James, who lives in West Adams, supplies Nancy with weed and sage parenting advice. She is the sanest person in Nancy's life, and has the healthiest, most honest relationship with her family, until Nancy colludes with her nephew Conrad and starts a grow business behind her back. As you watch these families grapple with the harsh realities of their lives, you can't help but consider such questions as: Can you be a good mother and deal dope? Does being a moral crusader make a person a better mother than being a drug dealer? Are Nancy and Celia both morally bankrupt?

"As a drug it [weed] represents every dirty little secret behind the closed doors of those little uniform boxes on the hillside."

"I'll never forget when Jenji first came into my office to pitch *Weeds*," says Danielle Gelber, senior vice president of original programming for Showtime Networks, Inc. "Jenji sat in a funky lotus position on my couch and told me about a high school friend whose mother dealt pot. Jenji told me how she wore a gorgeous designer blazer that was outfitted like a fisherman's or photographer's vest with all of these secret compartments. She was just padded with pot everywhere. Jenji obviously logged that in her brain over the course of her life, so she pitched that idea for the show. She had all of the characters, the scenario all planned out—everything. And it all became very real when we got the script, which was inarguably excellent. She delivered in a huge way."

"Weed" as a metaphor is the perfect gateway into this Agrestic world: It's a suburban scourge if ever there was one, a hearty little uninvited plant that pops up on a beautifully manicured lawn like a squatter and symbolizes the people and the problems that unexpectedly turn up, that isn't easily removed and reemerges often stronger and worse than before. As a drug it represents every dirty little secret behind the closed doors of those little uniform boxes on the hillside. Weed as a drug is innocuous enough to seem unthreatening—it would be hard to sympathize with Nancy if she was dealing crystal meth—but has the potential to grow into something big and unwieldy, and lead to other, more dangerous ventures. "The theme to the show is the bullshit we all live with," says Benabib. "It's about getting underneath it and seeing who we really are. Right now the culture is awash in bullshit. And people are less and less able to separate what's true from what's crap and what's self-delusional."

Weeds has garnered innumerable awards and nominations for writing, directing, editing, and acting, because it brilliantly evokes the dysfunction of an American suburb, but that has not limited its audience to the U.S. Not all American comedies work internationally, but *Weeds* has spread like, well, a weed, airing in 130 territories worldwide, according to Sandra Stern, COO of Lionsgate, which produces the series. "The humor from *Weeds* comes from characters and situations as opposed to set up the joke, laugh. Jokes don't necessarily translate into other cultures and other languages, but situations do." According to Kevin Beggs, president of production and programming for Lionsgate, viewers around the world love the show because of the way it both sends up our culture and portrays these lives with such candor. "I live in the suburbs of L.A. I know these people. I know these parents at the PTA. It's very real. Whether I was involved with the show or not, I would be watching this show repeatedly."

Everyone involved in the show—the cast, the writers, the crew, the network, the producers, the distributors—have become *Weeds* addicts, which only makes the series that much better, because each person is so invested in this grand collaboration. "I love the fact that we're actually producing a show that I look forward to watching and that my friends look forward to watching, and that I love to give as gifts to people because I'm so proud of it," says Stern. "I love all twelve of our television series, but I have to admit it, *Weeds* is my personal favorite."

Getting Kush-y with
JeNJI KoHan
Creator and Executive Producer of *Weeds*

Jenji Kohan—the series creator, executive producer, show runner, and head writer—talks about the business of dealing . . . with her cast and writing staff, suburbia, and, oh yeah, weed.

What inspired you to create a series about a hot, drug-dealing, suburban widowed mom?

I was really obsessed with shows like *The Shield* and *The Sopranos*, which have characters operating in the gray areas. There is a concept in psychology called "postconventional morality," which is the idea that when you're not following the rules of society, you have to develop your own moral code. I love the notion of a character having her own morality. I had to find my issue or the establishment that I would be up against, and drug dealing seemed like a really good premise. Pot was in the air in California with the passage of Proposition 215, the medical marijuana initiative. I came up with a one-line pitch about a suburban widow pot-dealing mom. I decided to make her a widow because it would make it easier to sympathize with her, and set it in suburbia because I was fascinated with the suburbs—my mother always said all of the interesting stories are in the valley. Pot was the perfect vehicle for the show because, while it is a Schedule I narcotic, it's not taken seriously, and it crosses every boundary. Every political affiliation, every gender, every class, every family has a pot smoker—it's all-access. That one-line pitch got me through the door at Showtime. After I sold them on the pitch, I was like, "Oh shit, how am I going to write this show?" I'm not a pot smoker—I'm too much of a control freak—and I had to learn about this world. When I actually sat down to write the pilot, though, it just sort of flowed all at once: all of these people in all of these situations.

The show's title, *Weeds*, appears to have as many metaphoric meanings as it does literal ones in this series.

Yeah, it certainly represents the characters in Nancy's life. Weeds are hardy little plants that grow despite all of your best efforts to kill them, and flourish in the most unlikely circumstances.

Half of the people in Nancy's life crop up like weeds, as do the occupational hazards of her new job, which invites compromising, even harrowing situations. The business of selling pot is weedlike—ever-growing, unwieldy, impossible to stop.

Exactly. Nancy, a woman in her forties who lacks practical skills, has not been in the job market and has never had a "career" per se. She suddenly discovers that dealing pot is something she's good at doing. What is someone who is suddenly in her situation going to do when she and her kids are used to living a certain lifestyle? For her, dealing pot is the perfect solution. But I also think that in her grief, she's not making the best decisions. She's not thinking things through, but I think once she sets off, the momentum carries her.

As it turns out, Nancy is as reckless as she is alluring to everyone from Conrad to Peter, from Celia to her own kids. By the end of the second season she has unwittingly betrayed nearly everyone in her life, and her friendship with Celia, such as it was, comes undone. Still, with all the guns pointed at her in the last scene of the season finale, we want her to get out alive. What do you think it would take for viewers to lose sympathy with Nancy?

My hope is that as Nancy rationalizes her actions, the audience will rationalize along with her, as [I hope they will] with all of these characters. As writers, we've got to walk that fine line where we still like these people, or sympathize with them or root for them, even though they're doing really horrible things. Nancy is trouble. She is a succubus. But Nancy loves her children and will do anything for them, and part of her thinks she's become a dealer for them, to secure their future. Nancy is trying her best. She thinks she's doing the right thing. The truth is, who among us is the best parent in the world? We're all doing the best that we can. No one wants to be a bad parent. But there's another side to Nancy: She's a danger junkie, and she's latched on to something that makes her feel excited.

Where did Celia Hodes come from?

Celia just sort of presented herself on the page. I wanted the model of a moral compass in a weird way, and represent what was supposed to be but wasn't being served by that. I created her to be totally different from Nancy, someone who is doing everything she was always told she was supposed to be doing and it is not getting her anywhere and it is making her angrier. All the things she hoped for in her life just weren't coming true.

On the surface Celia Hodes can be an unrelenting bitch, but not hateful. In fact, we develop a soft spot for Celia when she's diagnosed with breast cancer, and learn the source of her exacting standards when we meet her narcissistic mother.

I think Celia's very sympathetic. Her meanness doesn't come from an evil place. It all comes from pain, though often Celia creates her own pain. But it is born out of her unfulfilled dreams and desires and frustration with how her life turned out. I think she was someone who expected a big life and got a small one. Our choice to have Celia go through breast cancer and change and then ultimately return to exactly who she was before is the idea that people don't change at all. We all make the same mistakes over and over — we are who we are. I don't know if it's true or not, but that was this character's journey. We returned her to exactly where she started, which is not a good place.

Isabel Hodes is a resilient kid, emerging stronger than ever after her mother swaps out her chocolates for laxatives.

I love Isabel—she is terrific and somehow gained a strong sense of self somewhere along the way. Her dad loves her unconditionally and adores her and thinks the sun rises and sets on her. I think she was able to garner strength from that. And Allie Grant is just amazing. I've been so blessed with the casting choices for the show.

In the second season, the already tenuous friendship between Celia and Nancy comes to a head, literally, when Celia pulls Nancy's hair and demands that she be her friend. Why did you decide to break them up?

We always say of Celia and Nancy that they gravitate toward each other because they are probably the two brightest women in Agrestic, and even though they wouldn't necessarily have chosen each other as friends, they are what the other one has in this circumstance. There is also a sibling quality to their relationship, so we decided they would have a screwy, hair-pulling odyssey of a fight. In the original draft of the script, which was written by [story editor] Rolin Jones, there was no fight between Celia and Nancy, and we were looking for something, because we had this growing tension between the two. We were really happy with how it turned out. It's funny: We're constantly asked why Nancy and Celia can't be better friends. They're competitive and they're in each other's lives. I don't know that I'd call it a close friendship. Neither really knows how to be friends with other women. We were joking that Celia was queen of the dipshits and she wants to be

in with the cool crowd. To Celia, Nancy is real and different and could possibly show her a way to be real and different, but she grows increasingly frustrated with Nancy, and she knows there's something going on—she's not quite sure what it is, but she feels like she's being left out. She thought their friendship might have been more than it was. What she doesn't realize is that Nancy is isolating herself from any kind of female companionship. I think it's something missing from her life.

Heylia James and her family are the least neurotic people in Nancy's life. Heylia is at once a shrewd businesswoman, a tough-loving mother, and a romantic, qualities she seems to have passed on to her daughter, Vaneeta, who is poised to take over the family business. Conrad is a visionary and an honest man with a plan, despite his susceptibility to Nancy's charms. Were they inspired by anyone in your life?

I used to spend a lot of time in Venice Beach playing dominoes when [supervising producer] Devon Shepard and I were writing for *The Fresh Prince of Bel-Air*. The guys who were playing down there were a motley crew—really edgy. I started keeping score. The rule was, when you kept score, you could sit down at the next seat, but people kept cutting in front of me and wouldn't let me sit down and play. But I kept coming back. I finally got to sit down and they realized I could play. After that I went down all the time. This was during the O.J. trial, and there were a lot of frank conversations at the tables about that. I had a relationship with these guys like the one Nancy has with Heylia's family, and I loved them. They were scary and crazy, and they were my guys that I played with. I got a pass to operate there and be a fly on the wall. So Heylia and her family are kind of an homage to that time in my life and those guys.

During the first season, some critics called you on the carpet for your depiction of black characters, and even for the fact of your writing them at all.

We've come under attack: How can this white girl write this black family? Blah-blah-blah. No, I'm not black, but these are people I know and understand, and this is how they talk. What's up with the "I could never understand a black person, or know a black person, or know how they sound"? That's kind of offensive. Can men not write female characters? Can Jews not write non-Jews? Fuck that. I spent so much time with these guys at Venice Beach. I *knew* them, and this is my experience of how they spoke and how they related.

We get to know the James family like we get to know the Botwins and the Hodeses. I don't apologize for a second. I think they're a terrific family, a functional family unit, and I think they're the heart of the show. I'm proud of these characters and what they do. I love all of my characters.

What are some of the biggest challenges you've faced in the past two seasons?

I was pregnant through the whole first season and gave birth on premiere night. I had two months off and then we went back for the second season, and I pumped breast milk every day and the nanny came and picked it up. So Oscar is our little *Weeds* baby. Because we shoot from April to July, and we're in post-production until the beginning of September, I miss the whole summer with the kids, and that has been really hard. Really hard. The biggest challenge in writing has been balancing humor and drama, although we don't let it bother us. If a moment is dramatic, we go for it. If it is funny, we go for it. We don't pull our punches anywhere. Really, the hardest thing about writing this is the hardest thing about writing: getting your ass in the chair and doing it well. Having a story to tell and telling it in a relatable fashion. And, with a television series, sometimes you set out to do things that don't always turn out the way you thought they would. Our cancer story line was very much an homage to [co–executive producer] Roberto Benabib's wife, who died from cancer. Elizabeth Perkins wasn't comfortable with certain aspects of our cancer story, and we got stress in general, so we might have pulled back on some things we didn't want to. I would have also liked to explore the religious themes more in the second season, with Andy in rabbinical school, but we were on such a trajectory with all of the other stories that we kind of flew off the train a little bit. Some things worked out beyond our expectations and other things fell a little short. That's making television. It goes very quickly and you have to be able to let go, and we write and we adjust. But for the most part, we stick to our game plan.

Weeds is praised for, among other things, its grit and candor, and a lot of it comes from the dialogue. Does that make your cast squeamish?

The first season the actresses were scared of the material and afraid that this was a career killer. We were asking people to say really edgy things, and we lost some jokes and some lines. There were a lot of struggles and battles because no one knew how the show was going to be received. We had to gain people's trust, and ensure that they weren't going to get killed for saying the words we were putting in their mouths. It wasn't easy. But I think once we got the positive attention that we got, and everyone's friends liked the show, it got a lot easier.

You had to cast this show from top to bottom, and you can't ask for a better roster of talent. Did any of the actors make you reconsider your initial idea of a character?

Justin Kirk gave me a different image of Andy. I had always intended to have the Andy Botwin character in the series—I had spoken about him in the pilot, and he had been part of the genesis in my notes. But we didn't get to meet him until the fourth episode of the first season, and we didn't yet have the actor. We'd been auditioning people all day, and Justin was the last one of the day. He came in and blew it out of the water. He *was* Andy. I had always envisioned Andy as more of a "dude," a dumb charmer, but Justin came in and did a completely different take. I liked his way; it was brilliant. Now Andy is so much more complicated, and brighter and more interesting. Justin is an extraordinarily gifted actor and a lovely person. He is filled with *ruach*! And Andy is so much fun to write.

What amazes you most about working on this series?

The people who work on it, from top to bottom—we are so blessed! They get the show and they love the show and there really isn't a weak link. Even our grips will take meal penalties because we've got to get it done. If we can't afford to go out and shoot, our line producer, Mark Burley, will find a place in the neighborhood. He always makes it work. Every department is filled with people who are good at their jobs. They get it. They get it right, often on the first time. It's so exciting. We live and die by our details. We are really watching every little second because we only have thirty minutes and we want to pack them.

In the Weeds with

nancy BOTWIN:

The Suburban Baroness of Bud

THE DOPE on ...
nancy

Ever since her forty-year-old husband, Judah Botwin (see "Nancy Botwin's Kif and Kin: The Dead Husband: Judah Botwin"), died of a heart attack and left Nancy with two traumatized sons and an empty savings account in the nouveau riche Los Angeles private community of Agrestic, the young widow has found that the whole landscape of her life is suddenly overrun with weeds. Perhaps it's an occupational hazard of living in the suburbs—and of becoming Agrestic's baroness of bud.

BOTWIN

Nancy never set out to become a dealer, at least not at first. She just sort of fell into it after her stoner brother-in-law, Andy, put her in touch with his old pal Conrad Shepard, thinking she'd want to take the edge off her grief with some smoke. But Nancy saw how much her friends were enjoying her pot, and then considered how few discernible career skills she had. Dealing weed struck her as a viable solution to all of her immediate problems. She could maintain her role as watchful soccer mom to teenage Silas and pre-pubescent Shane because it would afford her the time and the money to preserve a sense of normalcy and stability in their crazy home, allow her to hold on to the capacious house and the lease on the Range Rover, and enable her to keep their beloved housekeeper, Lupita, on the payroll. And she would be providing a discreet service to the local tokin' community. Just how much risk it will involve—her sanity, her life, other people's lives— won't fully reveal itself until she's thick in the weeds.

It never fails to shock a PTA mom like Nancy how quickly she's become the "big-gest game in the private community of Agrestic" ("You Can't Miss the Bear") just from selling dime bags to acquaintances—Judah's poker buddies, lawyer Dean Hodes, and accountant/city councilman Doug Wilson, as well as people such as Shane's karate coach. But as her supplier, Heylia James, tells her, "Drugs sell themselves, biscuit. You ain't shit" ("You Can't Miss the Bear"). Nancy's greatest initial concern is being found out by her kids, the "hypo-Christian bitch moms" of the PTA ("Fashion of the Christ"), and her neighbor and unlikely friend, PTA president Celia Hodes, who loves her martinis but has an intense hatred for marijuana. Only when she is pulled under the kitchen table during a shootout at Heylia's house does it occur to Nancy that "the downside to this business is death" ("'Lude Awakening").

Nancy is feeling so bereft that it requires a blaze of bullets to awaken her from her daze. Her overwhelming loneliness and heartache often render Nancy speechless, and particularly incapable of opening herself up to those who reach out to her, like her business partner, Conrad; her parasitic brother-in-law, Andy; her shell-shocked kids; and her neighbor Celia Hodes, who is eager to be her friend. Other times, Nancy's suppressed grief explodes into rage, like when she smashes the family's digital video camera onto the patio ground, shattering it into pieces. Yet she allows herself to weep with longing in the privacy of her bedroom as she watches videos of Judah making love to her. Most days

she focuses on holding it together and tending to family problems she can resolve: paying outstanding utility bills, bailing Shane out of trouble with Principal Dodge (played by David Doty), and reining in Andy, who "turns [everything] to shit" with the touch of his hand ("Fashion of the Christ"). But mornings are the hardest. After nights of dreaming memories of a peaceful existence with her husband, Nancy is jolted awake by the realization of her very real nightmare: that life will never again include Judah.

Nancy is aware that her emotional reserve and increasing unavailability to her kids has repercussions, though she feels helpless to do anything about it. She often worries that the wrong parent has died, and confesses her darkest, most guilt-ridden fantasy to Conrad: "I love my kids more than anything. . . . But sometimes I think about what it would have been like if they had died when Judah died. What it would be like to not have to worry. To be only responsible for me. And free. How nice that might feel. How horrible is that? I'm an awful, horrible person. . . . I love my kids. They're my life" ("Must Find Toes").

Silas, who can't bear his mother's distance and has figured out what Nancy does for a living, immerses himself in his relationship with Megan Beals (see "Silas Botwin's Special Bud: Megan Beals"), and seeks solace from her warm, welcoming family. Desperate not to

lose that connection, Silas intentionally impregnates an unwitting Megan after she gets accepted to Princeton; but his plan backfires when the family permanently and violently casts him out. After having deflected his feelings for two years, Silas is suddenly overwhelmed with grief for everyone who has left his life, and for the life he used to have. He yearns more than ever for Nancy's attention. As far as he can tell, the only way to be around her is to work for her. But Nancy holds her ground. He decides to protect her instead by dismantling the surveillance cameras from Celia's community-wide antidrug campaign. But in a bitter twist of irony, Silas puts her life at greater risk.

Nancy's younger son, Shane, is being relentlessly teased at school, where his peers call him "Strange" Botwin. He has always skewed odd, but since witnessing his father's fatal heart attack, he's been acting out in increasingly disturbing ways—Principal Dodge practically has Nancy on speed dial. But he's the only Botwin allowing himself to mourn in the moment. At home Nancy can usually find Shane sitting up in the rafters, watching old footage of his father on the family's video camera, or plopped in front of the TV with Lupita, eating ice cream. But he's been spacing out in the middle of his soccer games and subsequently getting kicked by his teammates; writing murderous gangsta raps; filming a terrorist video evocative of Daniel Pearl's assassination; shooting a mountain lion with a BB gun; trying to cre-

ate a real burning bush on school grounds using his father's Zippo; and biting his karate opponent at a tournament—at least *that* leads to Nancy meeting a handsome single dad, Peter Scottson. Nancy actually considers Shane's demand to be put on Paxil before Andy convinces her to keep the kids off drugs—prescribed ones, anyway. Handling Shane is one of the only benefits Andy provides Nancy—he has a way with his nephew, which comes in especially handy when puberty rolls around.

Most days Andy is a persistent, proliferating weed in Nancy's life, who springs up in her kitchen one morning, attempts to assume Judah's place in the family with none of the responsibility, and nearly ruins her and her business with his carelessness. And he even has the gall to call her "Pants"—Judah's nickname for her. Not cool. Out of familial obligation, Nancy gives Andy free room and board, bails him out of jail for possession and pays his legal fees, covers his tuition for rabbinical school so he can dodge his tour of duty in Iraq, and includes him as a partner in her grow business. In return he contrives ways to cut in on her business, threatens to blow her cover to the boys, and nearly exposes her in the grow house neighborhood when he orders cable and DSL under her real name. He drops out of the rabbinate, hits on Silas's girlfriend, shows Shane how to use nunchaku, jeopardizes Shane's only friendship by sleeping with the boy's mother, and helps himself to Nancy's stash and her friend Doug Wilson. And worst of all, he lets into their home Kat (see "Andy Botwin's Special Buds: Kat"), a crazy ex-girlfriend who will eventually kidnap Shane and head to Paraguay. And these are just the problems of which Nancy is aware. Andy is the furthest thing from Judah, and she can't help but wonder, "How did [Andy] and Judah emerge from the same mother?" ("Fashion of the Christ").

Nancy could really use a friend to lean on, but she has to be very careful who she trusts as her life becomes increasingly split in two. Nancy has to keep Celia at arm's length even as her neighbor aggressively campaigns for the role of her confidante. Celia is abra-

sive, needy, and incredibly sad—her marriage to Dean is in shambles; her house is destroyed by a Cessna; she battles breast cancer, perpetual loneliness, and persistent disappointment—but she stands out among the Stepford wives, and that appeals to Nancy. Celia also drinks, has a wicked sense of humor, and has a talent for dishing, which makes hanging out with her lots of fun, even though her unrelenting approach to parenting unnerves Nancy, as she witnesses when Silas is involved with Celia's daughter, Quinn (see "Celia Hodes's Kif and Kin: The Older Daughter: Quinn Hodes"). Celia believes all kids live to deceive; Nancy prefers to cleave to her naïveté. But with all the information that Celia possesses, it amazes Nancy that the PTA president is the only person in all of Agrestic who isn't apprised of her new career. And it must remain that way, especially since Dean is one of her secret clients; a co-conspirator alongside Doug in her money-laundering sham bakery, Breadsticks & Scones, and a silent partner in her grow business with Conrad. When Celia wrests

the city council seat from Doug, she launches a fierce antidrug campaign that dooms the potential for a substantive friendship. The more elusive Nancy becomes, the more Celia begs her to declare herself. "Aren't we friends? You can't even say it. You don't want to be my friend," Celia says. "Everything isn't about you," says Nancy, words that set Celia flying off the rails. She pulls a chunk of Nancy's hair and yells, "BE MY FRIEND! BE MY FRIEND!" ("Mrs. Botwin's Neighborhood"). Nothing can get Nancy away from Celia fast enough. Just wait until Celia steals Pam Gruber's gun!

Nancy gets her weed and wisdom from Heylia James, a tough-talking matriarch lording over a family of dealers in West Adams, an inner-city neighborhood just outside of Agrestic. Heylia becomes an accidental mentor to "Lilywhite" Nancy, imparting indispensable, often humbling business and parenting advice that feels as sharp and punitive as a slap in the face. "Every time I leave here, I feel like such an asshole," says Nancy ("Higher Education"). But Heylia, her daughter, Vaneeta, and her nephew Conrad are the only dependable, sane people in Nancy's life. While Nancy doesn't smoke pot, she does

get off on her secret life as a dealer — especially when she adopts a pseudonym, "Lacy LaPlante," to rent the grow house. She's discovered not only that she's good at something, but that peril is the greatest high she's ever known. Heylia and Vaneeta are shrewd businesswomen, and they sense this about Nancy; while they are all intrigued by their client and

sensitive to her predicament as a widowed mother, they approach her with caution because her strain of naïveté and recklessness has the potential to take everybody down.

Heylia's gorgeous, kindhearted nephew Conrad approaches with less caution because he's smitten with Nancy from the moment they first meet in Heylia's kitchen. He's a smart guy and yearns to become her guardian angel, frequently softening the blow of his aunt's strong words, often doing so behind her back. At first Nancy resists Conrad's overtures as she does everyone who tries to come near her, but his platonic companionship becomes impossible to resist, and the protection he provides her a necessity of life. Conrad helps her navigate the new world, dodging obstacles like cannabis clubs—the "Whole Foods of pot" ("Good Shit Lollipop")—and the violent competition as she cultivates her business from a one-woman dime-bag operation to an army of math geek dealers led by her son's tutor, Sanjay, at commuter college Valley State. Heylia calls Conrad out for fighting Nancy's battles when he beats up a corrupt security guard who jacks her stash, and she forbids him to talk to Nancy. When Conrad realizes Heylia is thwarting his growth in the business—she dismisses his innovative plans to expand their operation to hydroponic farming—he makes a bold, clandestine plan with Nancy to spin off on their own, which costs him his connection to his family. He brings the hash, and she has the cash, along with a team of business partners that include Dean,

Doug, Sanjay, former competing dealer Alejandro Rivera (see "Nancy Botwin's Contact Highs: The Head of Distribution: Alejandro Rivera"), and, begrudgingly, the "Yentl," Andy. They're good to grow.

The endeavor exceeds their expectations. Conrad's hydro—christened MILF Weed by Snoop Dogg, who thinks the weed is as fine as Nancy—becomes the hottest strain on the streets, but not without a roller coaster ride along the way. Just as they're settling in to the new grow house, which is tucked away in a residential cul-de-sac, they are welcomed by their neighbor Aram Kesheshian (see "Nancy Botwin's Obstacle Courses: Aram Kesheshian"), the head of the Northside Armenian Power, who welcomes them to the block with a going-away box of baklava.

The Armenian mafia turns out to be the least of their problems. After weeks of fending him off, Nancy gets involved with Peter Scottson, the adorable single father she met at Shane's karate tournament, only to discover that he's a DEA agent and that

he knows she's a purveyor of pot—but he's not yet aware that her game is getting bigger by the day. He's fallen in love with Nancy and gets her to elope with him to Las Vegas. Though it's a secret business arrangement that will protect Nancy from him testifying against her, he's hoping she and the marriage will both eventually turn legitimate.

Conrad learns of the liaison after the DEA takes care of the Armenians with a huge drug raid that clears the block and skips over their grow house. "Heylia was right," Conrad yells. "You open those big brown eyes of yours, and I fall into shit!" ("Crush Girl Love Panic"). When Nancy tips off Heylia about the DEA's plan to bust her to get to West Adams's most menacing dealer, U-Turn (see "Nancy Botwin's Obstacle Courses: U-Turn"), Peter realizes Nancy is never going to hold up her end of the bargain and start getting out of the business, and he starts to turn on her. Convinced that she and Conrad are having an affair, he taps her phone and overhears them refer to him as Agent Wonderbread. He is wrecked when Nancy confesses to Conrad, "I don't love [Peter] and I'm never going to love him" ("Mile Deep and a Foot Wide"), and, realizing that his career and—worse yet—his life are in jeopardy, he decides to seek revenge. Peter attacks Conrad and demands that they sell off their last harvest of MILF Weed, hand him all the money, and disappear from his life forever. Unbeknownst to Nancy, Heylia has a different idea of how the deal will go down, and it involves the Armenians and the offing of Peter. But Silas unwittingly puts everyone's life on the line when he runs away with all of the MILF Weed and tries to negotiate with his mother, while she is standing in the grow house kitchen with five gangsters pointing semiautomatics at her head.

HASHING IT OUT WITH . . .
mary-louise parker

What did you think of Nancy Botwin when you first read the pilot script?

I think you always get a hint of a character: Sometimes it's the rhythm of their speech, sometimes just the tone of the piece itself, and sometimes it's a particular line that jumps out at you or a moment that you have a kind of attachment to that gives you a pull to the character. There were a few moments in the script that really attracted me. I don't know if I felt that I saw a full person in my head so much as I felt like it was something that was evolving and continued to evolve. There were a lot of things I initially thought that I don't see anymore, but I do continue to think she's somewhat haunted and a bit lost [*laughs*].

Weeds **set decorator Julie Bolder described a vivid backstory you imagined for Nancy as you discussed her home, especially certain items that should appear in her bedroom and bathroom. She said you imagined Nancy as a onetime dancer and the family photographer when Judah was alive. How did you use this background information to enter into the Nancy we meet?**

It comes up in my favorite thing that I shot the first season, which we didn't use. It was an improv—and I'm not an actor who actually likes improv. I went to drama school for four years, and I'm kind of in line with Ingmar Bergman, so improvisation makes me dizzy [*laughs*]. So I did an improv with Jeffrey Dean Morgan, who played Judah, and it was centered around the day he got the video camera. I wanted her to be watching old videos and happen upon the one of them having sex, so I wanted to shoot some other home movies of the two of them. I had them shoot the day she gave him the gift of the video camera. Jeffrey and I talked ahead of time about what we were going to do: With improv you have a skeleton and then you kind of let go. I said I would do ballet for him but I didn't want to, so it was him filming me doing ballet, and then he came into the frame—he set down the camera—and we were in it together; it was all very rough and raw. Jeffrey was wonderful—he was so engaged. He was the best possible actor to improv with because he was open and positive and he just went with me and I loved it.

When we first meet Nancy, she is only selling weed to people she knows, such as her husband's poker buddies and [her son] Shane's karate teacher. Once she discovers she's got a knack for it, however, she starts building her "pyramid," which consumes more and more of her attention, time, and energy. What do you think about her growing attraction to dealing and danger?

In some ways, I feel like her character is experiencing a bit of a devolution, mentally, because she's become more reckless. She has so much more at stake, so much more to lose, and she's putting her children at risk. In that sense, I feel like, though her business is evolving, she's kind of careening out of control. I think she would love for someone to step in and stop her.

Perhaps that's what initially drew her to Peter.

Yeah, but he's the wrong guy.

Everyone who is ever bewitched by Nancy becomes the wrong guy because, to paraphrase Conrad, they all step in shit. As a widow and a mother, she is irresistible and sympathetic, and often her recklessness is mistaken for naïveté. What do you think it would take for people to stop connecting with her?

That's a really, really good question. But I don't know because I can't really ever care as an actor what investment people have in my character. I can only care whether or not I feel like I am presenting her as realistically as possible so that she'll seem like a person and not an actress. That's what I try to work at the hardest to present, even if that's something that seems boring or unsexy or silly.

This is the first time you've taken on a leading role in a television series. What do you do to get into Nancy's state of mind week after week, and between the seasons?

There are very specific things that are part of the person I like to create—her clothes, her shoes, her jewelry, her hair—that aren't mine. Those aren't my clothes. It's sort of something that's kind of mishmashed together. It's little things, the perfume that she wears. It's the actors that you work with who will bring you back into that world. The music that I listen to. Hopefully it comes together and there will be some kind of continuity and inevitably I will disappoint myself wildly [laughs] and I'll just try to keep searching and trying to make it better.

I know music is very important to you. Is there an interior soundtrack that you have that gets you in the Nancy state of mind?

Yes. I based the character on part of a song. Leona Naess's music really speaks to my character. I asked [the producers] to use her as a backdrop for some of Nancy's scenes. There was one scene in the first year, I had it in my head for the scene and I asked them to use it, and I got the rights to it from Leona.

As a mother, is it hard to play a careless parent?

No, it's fun. I certainly don't draw from my own experience [laughs]. She's decidedly spiritually and emotionally disorganized, and she lives in a world of mental clutter. Her parenting is skewed at the moment. I think that she would like to parent better. I just don't think she's a natural parent. I've wanted to be a parent my entire life, and I think it comes kind of naturally to me. I think it doesn't come naturally to some people. I decided Judah was the better parent and I told Jenji. She liked that idea and was very open to it.

Do you like Nancy?

I don't think about it because it's not like I'm going to hang out with her. Do you know what I mean? I'm just into the minutiae, creating her as a person. I'm so far into her, [but] if I really stopped to think about it, would I be friends with her? Probably not. No. I don't think we have the same taste. I don't think we'd go to the same movies. It doesn't matter to me whether I like my characters or not. I don't construct them under those terms of like or dislike. I'm too myopic for that, and I can't step back far enough to be able to ask myself that question. And I also don't take it lightly enough to be able to ask myself that.

You've embellished Nancy's character, like giving her a coffee habit, which makes her even more vivid. Are there other ways you've helped shape her throughout the series?

If you watch the choices that I make, I do it myself in the course of the scene—like she will reach for a Diet Coke for breakfast, those kinds of little choices. Then there are internal choices that are private that are the kind of things that are the most important choices that I could never tell anyone.

Was there a scene that was especially hard to do, one that you found especially emotionally grueling, or hard to pin down?

The scene in "Bash," when I beat the piñata, though they ended up cutting so much out of it. It was actually much more grueling. I had this whole monologue to Silas, so it was really hard when I shot it. That was pretty intense, though it was more intense to watch when I saw what was cut out of it [*laughs*]. You were supposed to see the piñata open and all the Almond Joys come out.

What's it like working with your on-screen sons, Hunter Parrish and Alexander Gould?

I love them. I thought Hunter really blossomed this year in such a wonderful way and surprised me so many times. He took it so seriously and came at it in an interesting way. I was really proud of him. I have a very protective [*laughs*], loving, wonderful relationship with Hunter. The scenes with [Megan played by] Shoshanna Stern were fantastic. She brought the level of the show up a notch, I thought, just by showing up. I think she's deeply gifted. And Alexander is just an angel. He is so sweet. You kind of want to keep him frozen in time.

This is your fourth project with Martin Donovan. He tells me you got him this job.

Yes, and I tell Martin [*laughs*] that I take complete and full credit for every brilliant moment that he has because of that [*laughs*]. I love him so much. There are just some people that I have worked with, like him and John Turturro, where we just work the same way, and it's totally easy for me. It's wonderful for me to have him around. And Justin Kirk is the same way.

When Andy first crash-lands at the Botwin household, Nancy is exasperated, but he seems to have ingratiated his way into her heart.

I think she and Andy have an enormous love.

One of my favorite scenes with Nancy and Andy together is in "Crush Girl Love Panic," when they are both outside of Silas's door. She is trying to coax Silas out of his room with the karaoke machine, and Andy is explaining the invasion of Panama to Shane. It's hilarious in its depiction of this dysfunctional parenting unit, while perfectly portraying the amazing chemistry you and Justin share.

It's interesting: A lot of people have mentioned that scene to me, about the chemistry between Justin and me. He and I have spent a lot of time together, obviously, from having worked together in *Angels in America*. I love to work with him. I wish I had more with him. I can't take credit for Justin as I can with Martin—I wish I could.

This season Nancy gets permission to be a badass once she is given an alternate identity.

That's exactly right. It sanctions her misbehavior. I wish there were more places for that because I feel like that got lost a little bit this season, and I think Jenji agreed with me that Nancy got lost there a little. It's most interesting to me when she kind of veers outside of the social roles she's supposed to follow. I don't think she's the brightest person in the world. I think she can be savvy and I think she has moments of wisdom in spite of herself. It's curious to me. I'm still trying to figure that out, to what level. She is smart in moments, but that doesn't make her intelligent. I don't think she is very good at self-examination and I don't think she thinks very far beyond the next twenty minutes. I think that's her greatest downfall. I think maybe when forced to, you may find a little bit of wisdom there. I don't even know how kind she is, except maybe to her children. She's extremely narcissistic, but I also think she's charming. I think she's trying hard and that makes her appealing. But I think Celia is a much nicer person.

Some of the series's most mordantly humorous—and certainly the most combative—moments emerge in scenes between Nancy and Celia. You and Elizabeth are fantastic together.

I love her. I was most excited when they said she was going to do the show. It doesn't get any better than her. In the hands of any other actress, Celia would have had maybe one-and-a-half dimensions. And she's also extraordinarily cool and funny and the kind of woman that you want to walk into the camper at five in the morning or two in the afternoon. She is really, really special and I wish I had more scenes with her. They [the producers] said that in season three I will, so I'm hoping that it's the case. Who knows what's going to happen? The end of the second season was pretty crazy. I was left standing there with my Diet Coke.

No one can humble Nancy quite like Heylia James and Vaneeta. Tonye and Indigo both bring a lot of warmth to the table.

I love doing scenes in that house. I love Indigo and Romany and Tonye. She is a loving and incredible woman. She's got a great spirit and she's generous with me. There is not a single lemon in the bunch. That's pretty hard to believe. I have affection for all of them: Renée Victor [who plays Lupita], Maulik Pancholy [Sanjay], and Allie Grant [Isabel]. They aren't there every day but they add a lot to the show.

Is there one scene that felt like your truest Nancy moment?

I think the scene in "The Punishment Light," where she's at the stoplight, and Peter calls. Because I think she falls into her body for a second, which she doesn't do very often. She really has a moment of realizing how ridiculous she is, because she's just had sex with a drug dealer in an alley and she's telling this guy she can't be intimate. I wanted to play that scene as being very extreme. It was just written as a conversation, like this guy calling her to say, "I'd really like to see you," and I was supposed to say, "I'm really not ready to get intimate," and I just saw it as being kind of explosive, like, well, the way I did it, that's how I saw it. What was your favorite episode in season two?

"Yeah. Like Tomatoes," because of the way Nancy gets yanked back into Botwin family reality, and it sobers her up if only briefly. She finally tells Shane what she does for a living, and then she discovers Silas has stolen all of the surveillance cameras, the drug-free zone signs, and the Sober the Sasquatch mask, and she realizes how bad things have gotten with him. How about yours?

That was my favorite, too. I also really like the scene [from "Must Find Toes"] in the grow house with Romany, where I smoke pot with him, because he was extraordinary in it. I loved sharing that scene with him. I felt like we gave the scene to each other. In season one, I loved "The Punishment Light." That was when Nancy was completely out of control. But it added up to something. There was almost a benediction at the end of that scene. I bought it—it felt true to me.

What would you like to see happen to Nancy?

The bigger, the crazier, the weirder, the better. I like it when she gets out of control. I don't want to be standing around in the grow house asking, "What should we do, guys?" Those were my least favorite. They take forever to shoot. We called [the grow house] the "slow house" [*laughs*]. If I didn't love those actors, it would have been interminable for me. But Andy Milder [who plays Dean Hodes] and Kevin Nealon [who plays Doug Wilson]—it's really boring to hear how much I love them, but I really love them all [*laughs*]. That's my little testimonial to the people of *Weeds*.

MARY-LOUISE PARKER is a multi-award-winning film, television, and theater actress. Her work on *Weeds* has earned her a Golden Globe Award and another nomination, and two SAG nominations for Outstanding Performance in a Comedy. Parker also won a Golden Globe, an Emmy Award, and a SAG nomination for her supporting role in Mike Nichols's highly acclaimed production of Tony Kushner's *Angels in America* for HBO, and an Emmy nomination for her performance on NBC's *The West Wing*. She has appeared in more than thirty films on the big and small screens, and stars opposite Brad Pitt in *The Assassination of Jesse James by the Coward Robert Ford*. Parker also boasts an extensive stage career, garnering innumerable nominations and awards for her performances in *Prelude to a Kiss*, *How I Learned to Drive*, *Reckless*, and *Proof*, which earned her a Tony, a Drama Desk Award, and the Outer Critics Circle, Drama League, Lucille Lortel, Obie, and *New York Magazine* awards. She also earned the 2001 T. Schrieber Studio's Outstanding Achievement Award. More recently she won the Philadelphia Film Festival Award for Career Achievement. Her personal and professional belongings, along with career memorabilia, are archived at the Howard Gotlieb Archival Research Center at Boston University, where she was the youngest person inducted to the society.

Nancy Botwin may be a suburban PTA mom with a Range Rover and a house made of ticky-tacky, but "Pants's" wardrobe doesn't quite jibe with the white-bread Agrestic aesthetic. Costume Designer Amy Stofsky talks about how she likes to funk with Nancy.

Nancy has the elegance of a dancer, but she has a subtle rock-chick edge. How would you describe her look?

Nancy maintains the funkiness of her youth, but it's a sophisticated funkiness. She's very California oriented in the old Laurel Canyon way, so I dress her in a lot of unconstructed clothing or clothing with a twist, leather jackets and cowboy boots, with a 1960s vibe. There isn't anything that doesn't work on Mary-Louise. She's very easy to fit, and she's got carriage.

When you first read the script, did you have a clear sense in your mind of what Nancy Botwin would dress like?

Yeah. There was always a concept for Nancy. And I always felt like there had to be something from Nancy's past that would suggest she'd go into this line of work. It doesn't come from somebody who is sheltered. I'm not saying that she did a lot of drugs or anything like that, but there was life that she saw before Agrestic.

Where do you find Nancy-wear?

I like to go to specialty stores, and find things you won't see on every TV show. Nancy's different, so I want to find something that stands out, because she does—her taste and palette suggest a place beyond Agrestic.

Little Boxes on the Hillside: The Botwin House

A Conversation with Set Decorator
JULIE BOLDER

The houses in Agrestic may all be built just the same, but the interiors speak volumes about each individual owner. Set Decorator Julie Bolder talks about taking a uniformly created suburban home and tricking it out Nancy-style.

How detailed are the writers and producers when you discuss their characters' personal aesthetics?

They give me a general concept in the beginning. The whole production is moving so fast, so they'll give me the flavor and say, "We'd like to say this with this character," and it's my job to interpret it. I show them the sets before we shoot them. Sometimes they ask for an adjustment, then I'll have their approval and we'll proceed.

Nancy doesn't cook, and she sustains herself on caffeinated beverages, but we learn in the very first scene of the pilot that she has just had her kitchen redone.

Yeah, Nancy's big, beautiful kitchen just sits there, and Celia's fridge is packed full of Diet

Coke, but they both have all top-of-the-line stuff. You should see the houses on which theirs were based! People have gone so far beyond their means to buy them that there's no furniture. They're all barren and cold!

Do you and Mary-Louise discuss what Nancy might have in her home?

Yes. Mary-Louise has a backstory for Nancy: She envisioned Nancy as a former ballet dancer for a company in San Francisco, and a hippie. She wanted to bring these elements into her bedroom, so there are not only pictures of her traveling when she was married to Judah, but she also said she wanted a lot of pictures of her kids in there, and lots of games. She liked to play her sons' Game Boys. Mary-Louise also told me specific things that she wanted by her bathtub because Nancy is in there a lot. She really wanted to deepen her character in the set, especially in the bathroom.

Her bathroom is like her private sanctuary. We've seen Nancy sitting in the empty tub fully clothed, just to catch her breath after she is almost shot in Heylia's kitchen.

That bathroom is the center of her whole world. The paint colors are very serene. Mary-Louise said Nancy liked certain soaps and candles. She didn't want them to look like she just picked them up in a mall; but rather more eclectic, like she picked some of these up along the way, so we got Dr. Bronner's soap, because that specifically appealed to Nancy's hippie nature. The wine bottles lined up along the back of the tub were from wine she drank with Judah.

Do you like getting input from the cast?

Yeah, I thought it was really neat when Mary-Louise weighed in. She specifically requested the little refrigerator near the toilet, and the Buddha in her bedroom. Those were things that she really thought about after she saw the set, and we were happy to accommodate. But I get a lot of creative license. And I talk a lot with Jenji. As a decorator, I have to make something that is really character appropriate, asking myself questions like, "What would Nancy pick?" That's what ultimately informs the decisions I have to make.

THE DOPE on . . .

andy

Nancy Botwin's
Kif and Kin:
The Brother-in-Law

BOTWIN

When "fancy cookin' trouble," otherwise known as Judah's younger brother, Andy, descends on the Botwin household, he literally sets off the alarms—at least in Nancy's kitchen. He tries to soften the blow of his crash-landing by surprising the sleeping clan with a homemade deluxe eggs Florentine breakfast, and a duffel bag full of inappropriate gifts—a vibrator for Nancy, a stolen two-way pager for Silas, and nunchaku for Shane. Only the announcement of a quick departure will put Nancy's mind at ease. But Andy is threatening to stay until he's successfully dodged the U.S. Army Reserves, who've called on him to serve in Iraq, and his crazy ex-girlfriend, Kat (see "Andy Botwin's

Special Buds: Kat"), who stabbed him for "kicking one of her spirit animals" ("Yeah. Like Tomatoes"). In other words, he has no plans to leave. Lupita takes one disgusted look at him and conveys everyone's sentiments in one heel-turning gasp. "Oh, shit. You. I'm no cleaning up after his mess" ("Fashion of the Christ").

And Andy is leaving messes everywhere. Within days of his arrival, he is doing bong hits and having cybersex with Silas's deaf girlfriend, Megan (see "Silas Botwin's Special Bud: Megan Beals") at Silas's computer, claiming he was doing a favor for his nephew because he needed to be shown how to "treat [her] like everybody else, then [she'll] pop right open like a can of Pringles" ("Fashion of the Christ"). He sets Shane up for a suspension when he ditches him during a bust of their impromptu grammar school sale of Andy's homemade "Chris Died for Your Sins" T-shirts. And he's taken over the couch, spending the afternoons watching porn, smoking bowls, and making a new friend in Nancy's accountant, Doug Wilson. When he pays a visit to Conrad—his old partner in crime from Circuit City—he makes an accidental discovery that gives him a lifetime's worth of free passes with Nancy and ensures his stay in her home. Andy taunts her as he prepares dinner: "I got some great recipes when I was over at my friend Conrad's JOINT earlier today," he says smugly. "POT roast. Corned beef HASH. Tonight, though, I'm going Italian with a little BAKED ziti and a big plate of spaghetti MARIJUANA . . ." ("Fashion of the Christ").

Now that Andy knows Nancy's secret, he feels entitled to hone in on her business—after all, he gave her the hookup. When she refuses him, Andy resolves to start his own. But he's too indiscreet with the ounce he buys from Nancy's supplier—Conrad's aunt, Heylia James—which he samples in his rickety old blue van. He's immediately caught by a cop on a bike, who throws him in jail. Nancy bails him out if only because she is beginning to recognize him as a potential domestic asset—he's a great cook and Shane is crazy about him. So she hires him a hippie lawyer, Alannah Greenstein (see "Andy

Botwin's Special Buds: Alannah Greenstein, Attorney-at-Law"), who gets him off with a slap on the wrist if he agrees to attend Marijuana Anonymous. The twelve-step program doesn't exactly get Andy on the wagon, but it does win him a night of hot stoner sex with his smokin' sponsor, Sharon (played by Brooke Langton). The secret to Andy is he can charm his way into and out of nearly everything.

Andy endears himself to Eileen Dodd (played by Clare Carey)—the mother of Max (played by Forrest Landis), Shane's only friend—with the attention he pays to the boys, and to the osso bucco he's preparing for dinner. He's rewarded with a rowdy affair that unfortunately leaves him with teeth marks. Nancy warns him against getting bored with Eileen. "My son finally finds a friend and you have to go fuck his mother. . . . You are going to continue fucking the biter until Shane and Max apply to separate colleges or you run out of soft tissue, whatever happens first. You made your bed, now fuck in it!" ("Higher Education").

He eventually charms his way into Nancy's business, first as her perpetually baked baker at the "fakery," Breadsticks & Scones, and then as one of her partners in her grow business with Conrad. It's the price she pays for the increasing amount of parenting duties he's taken on at home—he's far from ideal, but at least he's well intentioned and present. Silas eventually develops a brotherly relationship with Uncle Andy. Shane worships him. So when Nancy realizes that she can't pull off the puberty and masturbation conversation with her twelve-year-old without making them both feel squeamish, Uncle Andy happily steps up to the plate. He delivers an unforgettable lecture to an attentive if baffled Shane, about "jerkin' the gherkin," "polishing the raised scepter of love," and cleaning up "pearl jam." By the time Uncle Andy doles out the homework assignment—a banana—Shane is rarin' to go ("Last Tango in Agrestic"). Andy even takes Shane to a massage parlor to get his first hand job so that he won't get teased at school, though Nancy must *never* find out about that.

There isn't an immediate payday for his contributions, though. At the grow house Andy endures a terrifying DEA raid and loses two toes to Doug's new friend, a hungry, bling-clad pit bull named Mr. Sweaters. As Nancy hands out bonuses to each of the partners, she passes over her stunned brother-in-law. "Once you reimburse me for room and board and for a nonrefundable year of rabbinical school, and for the time I bailed you out when you got busted, not to mention the lawyer's fees, you'll be compensated," she explains. "I'm a contributing member of this team," Andy counters. "I cook!" ("MILF Money").

When the U.S. Army Reserves tracks him down in Agrestic and summons him for duty in Iraq, Andy delivers layers of charm as if his life depended on it . . . because it does. After discovering that "once you go rabbi, you never go bye-bye" ("The Godmother"), Andy begs his way into the good graces of Yael Hoffman (see "Andy Botwin's Special Buds: Yael Hoffman"), a sexy, steely veteran of the Israeli army who runs the office of admissions at Hadmirash L'Torah rabbinical school. Initially she blows him off. "You talk a lot, and yet you say nothing" ("Corn Snake"). But he gently wears her down, and she gives him an opportunity to explain himself in an essay, which earns him a provisional admission to the school. Not content to cut his losses, Andy is determined to seduce her. After Yael turns him down repeatedly since he's not her kind of man—"I like a man. Someone big and

strong, someone who can grow a beard. You're pretty and I could flip you like a pancake" ("A.K.A. The Plant")—Yael decides he possesses qualities she likes in a woman and dates him . . . provisionally, and makes him take it like a man.

Andy discovers that he has a purpose in life, and it is not in the rabbinate, which he drops out of after the toe-biting incident (the injury earns him an automatic lifetime pardon from the U.S. Armed Forces). Unfortunately, it takes the menacing return of his ex-girlfriend Kat to bring about his revelation. Loaded up on sockeye salmon and wired on Red Bull, Kat turns up at the Botwin house to "rescue" him and whisk him away on her fugitive adventures as she is pursued all over the northern hemisphere by an Inuit bounty hunter named Abumchuk (played by Robert Allen Mukes). But Andy doesn't want to go because he realizes "I've got a thing here." He tells an incredulous Kat, "I'm helping my sister-in-law. I'm taking care of these kids. I'm getting my shit together" ("Mile Deep and a Foot Wide"). He prefers the comparably quiet insanity of Nancy's world to Kat's "bat-shit nuts" ("Pittsburgh") madcap antics, even if he still loves her for being who she is. Andy has laid down roots with the people he's befriended, reconnecting with Conrad, finding a platonic soul mate in Doug, and most poignantly for him, filling Judah's shoes in the best way he can. Andy's noble claims are put to the ultimate test when Kat, who hates traveling alone, steals his van, kidnaps a smitten Shane, and makes way for Paraguay.

Andy Botwin's Special Buds

Yael Hoffman,
played by Meital Dohan

Andy Botwin has a rare talent for insinuating himself into desired situations through the fine art of bullshit. But Yael Hoffman, a sultry and cynical Israeli army veteran who works as the director of admissions at the rabbinical school to which he's applying, isn't susceptible to his particular brand of charm . . . at least, not right away. It happens slowly, first when she allows Andy five minutes to explain himself—he needs rabbinical school to avoid a tour of duty in Iraq—and then when she provisionally accepts him into the school after he turns in an intriguing, THC-addled, solipsistic essay in the shape of a Torah scroll. No sooner does she let him in than he attempts a similar tack to get into her panties. But Yael, whose last boyfriend—her commanding officer in the Israeli army—was killed by a Hamas suicide bomber, isn't attracted to Andy, but he does possess the qualities Yael likes in a woman, which is good enough for him. She takes him by surprise when she straps on a big black dildo and fucks him up the ass. Enraged at the news that he's dropping out of rabbinical school after his toes are bitten off by a pit bull, a more surefire ticket out of military service, she dumps Andy. "I thought you had ruach! You scrawny, selfish little pig!" screams Yael. "That dog should've bitten your dick off!" ("Must Find Toes").

MEITAL DOHAN is an Israeli film and television star. She has also guest starred on *The Sopranos.*

Kat, played by Zooey Deschanel

Andy first turned up at the Botwin house to hide from two forces greater than him: the U.S. Armed Forces and his crazy ex-girlfriend, Kat, whom he left back in Alaska after she tried to kill him by stabbing him with an icicle when she thought he kicked one of her spirit animals ("Yeah. Like Tomatoes"). She turns up on Nancy's doorstep with her unpublished memoir in hand—Permafuck: A Journal of Spirit Rape—after driving for forty-three hours straight,

sustaining herself on stolen cans of sockeye salmon and Red Bull. Kat claims she has come to save him from the monotony of suburbia—and she also needs him to sign a release form for the memoir. Her credibility quickly crumbles when Andy notices they are being stalked by a gargantuan Inuit named Abumchuk, who just happens to be a bounty hunter and Ultimate Fighter. Kat finally lets it slip that she's on the lam for having stolen $1.3 million worth of chips from a Canadian casino, and wants a partner in crime as she flees to Latin America. Andy has always adored her as much as he's been terrified of her—she makes him feel crazy and alive—but he is feeling strangely settled in Agrestic, and decidedly devoted to his family. Determined not to travel alone, Kat steals Andy's van and kidnaps love-struck Shane, and heads south to Paraguay.

ZOOEY DESCHANEL has appeared in many films, making her big debut in *Almost Famous*. She will be starring as Janis Joplin in the upcoming film *The Gospel According to Janis* and costars with Mary-Louise Parker in *The Assassination of Jesse James by the Coward Robert Ford*.

Alannah Greenstein, Attorney-at-Law,
played by Allison Janney

No sooner does Andy try his hand at dealing in Agrestic than he gets busted by a cop on a bike with the ounce he just bought from Heylia James. After bailing him out of jail, Nancy hires Andy a hippie, bong-collecting, pothead lawyer, Alannah Greenstein, who helps him get off on the charges with a slap on the wrist—he has to go to Marijuana Anonymous meetings (it's his first strike)—and gives Nancy indispensable advice on the federal and California marijuana laws as she plans her cover business, Breadsticks & Scones. Alannah commends Nancy's strategy, telling her, "If you can eat it, you can beat it. . . . It's not illegal to have weed—less than an ounce, that is—but it's illegal to buy it . . .
[and] as long as it's broken down, nonspecific weight, we're talkin' a slap on the wrist. Three to five years' probation." In case of emergency, she suggests fleeing to Mexico or Canada, where they have "primo weed and really good Chinese food" ("'Lude Awakening").

ALLISON JANNEY is a four-time Emmy-winning actress best known for her starring role in the television series *The West Wing*. She has also appeared in such films as *American Beauty*, *The Object of My Affection*, *Big Night*, *The Ice Storm*, *Primary Colors*, *Nurse Betty*, and *The Hours*, among many others.

HASHING IT OUT WITH . . .
JUSTIN KIRK

How do you make Andy so lovable and make his egregious behavior, especially in the first season, so forgivable?

Perhaps it speaks to my own lack of moral fortitude [*laughs*], but Andy doesn't seem to be harming anyone. Okay, he did leave Shane behind, but the principal had a whistle! There he is, looking for a place to crash for a while, and he discovers that his sister-in-law is in a business that he could see himself thriving in. He's not trying to fuck Nancy over, though in the first season it looked like he was. In his first episode it looked like he was going to turn Nancy in unless she cut him in on the deal, like Lupita. But he did say to Nancy, "No matter what you think of me, I love my brother and I have your back."

In his own weird way, he tries his best to be a good uncle.

Yeah. He truly believes he's helping Silas out with Megan [when Andy has online sex with her]. That was actually my favorite of the early scenes, where Andy convinces Silas to go try to get some [*laughs*]. It really felt like a love scene between an uncle and a nephew, where, from his perspective, he's trying to impart his wisdom, and if he gets a chance to jerk off in the meantime, so be it. There's not even a moment of shame. People love Andy. I don't judge. Hunter [Parrish] asked me, "Do you think your character changed from the first to the second season?" I said, "What do you mean?" And he said, "Well, I think he changed. I really hated him last year" [*laughs*]. Last year it was probably that he had these little one-off tricks, like fucking Shane's friend's mom or the girl at Marijuana Anonymous, or was shooting rats with Doug. In the second season he has more of an arc and full-on story line.

Andy is a slacker and a stoner, but he's far from dumb. Do you think he'll ever get it together?

I like how they make Andy extremely politically savvy, like he's been sitting reading blogs for years. There's no question that he's bright. He's a pleasure seeker. What would getting it together be for Andy? He's pursuing the things that he loves.

Before playing Andy, you were perhaps best known for your stunning performance as Prior Walter in Mike Nichols's production of *Angels in America* for HBO. Is Andy a lot different from other roles you've had?

Oh yeah. It's nice because for a long time I got cast in roles where I was sick, tortured, handicapped, or crying. I played the same character in two police procedurals: I played a guy who was locked up years ago and then, due to DNA evidence, they found out he was innocent, with Mariska Hargitay on *Law & Order: Special Victims Unit* and Anthony LaPaglia on *Without a Trace*. There must have been something about me that got me cast as the put-upon guy. To get this part in a comedy, and play this lover of life, is a real pleasure. I think *Weeds* is the greatest show in the history of television for, among other things, the fact that it has the ability to be the funniest and the saddest show. Our humor, as broad and silly and shocking as it can be, is never frat-boyish. It's smart. You don't get a bad taste in your mouth, even when Yael is strapping one on.

What was it like to deliver that masturbation lecture to Alexander Gould?

It was interesting [*laughs*]. When I was doing it I was thinking, how much of this is ringing true to him? The kid just turned twelve, so is this the kind of conversation I could be having with him in real life if I was his uncle? [*Laughs*] I couldn't tell you, because he pretty much came in and did his great little Alexander face and off he went. I was afraid that his parents thought I was really Andy. Alex's on-set teacher came up to me and said, "I want to thank you. You've been really appropriate with Alexander on the set. You had to do all this weird stuff." That was a relief. It's not me, it's the writers! [*Laughs*] Alex's little sister was on *Lucky Louie* on HBO, and I said to his mother, "Did you call your agent and say, 'Get my kids on the filthiest television series you can find'?" [*Laughs*] I really love Alexander—I have a great deal of affection for him.

You must have felt like you hit the jackpot when you first saw that monologue in the script. Supervising Producer Shawn Schepps said the writers spent hours online looking up every form and word for masturbation.

That makes sense, because I went to the writers when I got the script and asked, "Who the fuck came up with the banana?! Who has been doing it to a banana?" And one of them said, "I dunno. We found it on the Internet." [*Laughs*]

What do you think of Andy's scheme to use rabbinical school as a way station?

It seems to be his only option. And it sounds like it could be fun. He meets lovely Yael, who he becomes attached to. Now that his toes are gone, he thinks God may have a different plan for him. I don't see any malice. Is he letting God down? Is that the being he should feel guilty about? I think he's done his time for the Jews.

Andy gave his toes to the weeds cause. Did you, Justin, have to sacrifice anything for *Weeds?*

You know that scene where Nancy tells me I'm not going to get paid and then Silas and Andy are lying in the pool? I got sun damaged, and I still have these things on my torso. Hunter and I were in the pool, and we didn't get out in between setups because we needed to stay in one place, and we were being beaten on by the sun. We slathered on the sunscreen, but I guess I sweated it off just under the tits area [*laughs*] and then my belly button streaked. When I got out, I was fine—I wasn't burned at all. But when I went home and took my shirt off to get ready for bed, it looked like someone had finger-painted on me with pink paint. I was fish white like I normally am, except for these little streaks. I put aloe on and some stuff, and it gradually changed to a tan sort of color, but three months later, it's still there. It never blistered, and it never really hurt. I guess I should go to a dermatologist [*laughs*]. That's my *Weeds* tattoo.

Which scenes do you think best evoke the spirit of Andy?

In my very first episode I went from telling Silas how to make it happen with Megan to confronting Nancy about her line of work. As an actor I find you get credit for writing a lot of the time. "That was so amazing, that monologue about jerking off." I haven't been any better in an episode of a crappy show than in a good show. All we have is the story to tell.

What are some of the weirder things viewers have said to you when you've run into them?

A guy at a gas station came up to me and said, "Hey, you're on that show *Weeds*, right? I'm high right now" [*laughs*]. It's surprising how infrequently I'm offered weed. I thought it would become a thing where everyone would try to hook me up, but I guess everyone is so guarded with their stash.

Do you think Nancy is giving Andy a raw deal?

Yeah. I mean, Andy is man of the household. I may be too deep into this character [*laughs*], but the idea that she's not going to pay him, he just can't believe that shit. He's completely taken to Agrestic. He's cooking for the family. He's got a good friend in Doug. He's into the domesticity of it all. And he loves those kids, and it may point to the complexity of the relationship between him and his brother—there is reference to Judah being the golden boy and Andy being the fuckup—and now Andy has his family. It might sound a little creepy, but it means something to Andy, and he's found this world that he feels comfortable in. He's clearly a guy who likes adventure—he's always zooming off to Alaska and chasing whatever scheme—so why would he stay in Agrestic if it wasn't for these things? It's an interesting contrast with Nancy, because she is a danger junkie, and there is reference to the fact that she was like that before she met Judah, living as an artist on the fringe, and then she had the kids and made a suburban life of it. And every time something comes up, like the Armenians, for example, Nancy is the first one to say, "Fuck 'em. We have as much right to be here." She's on to the thrill of the next challenge.

When Kat [played by Zooey Deschanel] turns up at the Botwin household and tries to wrangle Andy back into her whacked-out world, he seems genuinely devoted to taking care of the family, and not just for the free greenery. She tries to call him on it.

Kat wants to think it isn't true so that Andy will join her on another journey of craziness because, as she says, "We had a real thing going," and she really liked him. In some ways, as upsetting as it was, they had very true energy together, and that's why, hon-estly, I don't know what's going to happen next. I better be nice to my bosses or they might send me off to Baja. That's exactly why they had Kat show up: to make Andy have to decide between the life that he lived and loved before and this newfound domesticity that is agreeing with him. I know that the writers' instincts are to not stay static in terms of the tone and the story line. They'd just as soon move us to a bizarre and different locale for the show. It's a job I really love. I love the actors and I am tight with the writers. It's a real blessing.

Who do you think is having better sex, Andy or Silas?

Andy is having some pretty good sex.

Do you think he liked Yael's special backdoor surprise?

I don't think there is any reason to believe that Andy didn't enjoy it. It's funny, we had a wider shot of Yael greasing up the dildo. You see her squirt lube, and her hand moving, but you couldn't see her actually lubing it up. Standards and Practices said, "You can't show that." That was the only time they reined us in [laughs]. We got so lucky with Meital—she is the real thing. I was reading with so many actresses, trying to find that part, but Meital is completely singular and perfect. She's loaded with *ruach* [laughs]. And she's such a sex kitten.

Who are some of your favorite characters on the show? Besides Andy, of course.

I have a soft spot for Dean. Heylia always has great stuff. Renée Victor is hilarious—Lupita makes me laugh as a viewer and as an actor. Indigo as Vaneeta is awesome. Everyone is spot-on for their parts. I love them all.

Andy gets some of the best lines in the series; among the most memorable is the setup for the coffee table joke.

That's the joke that rang like a shot heard around the world. People love that joke. It's almost like a great power pop song in that I swear I've heard it before [*laughs*]. Once you've heard it, you're like, "Oh, that's an old bit." Doesn't it seem like that? [*Laughs*] And then there's the baby arm line, when he's talking to Silas. I love that, because what seems at first blush to be sort of shocking or inappropriate is a genuine example of Andy's acceptance of different people in the world and encouragement to embrace things and go forward.

JUSTIN KIRK is best known for his Golden Globe–nominated role as Andy Botwin on *Weeds*, and his Emmy Award–nominated turn as Prior Walter in the television miniseries *Angels in America*, both opposite his *Weeds* costar Mary-Louise Parker. Kirk won the Obie Award for *Love! Valour! Compassion!* and went on to star in the film version of the play. His role in Jon Robin Baitz's *Ten Unknowns* at Lincoln Center won him a Lucille Lortel award, plus Drama Desk and Outer Critics Circle nominations. His other film credits include *Outpatient, Teddy Bears' Picnic, Chapter Zero, The Eden Myth, Puccini for Beginners,* and *Flannel Pajamas.* He has starred on television in the series *Jack & Jill* and guest starred in *The Pretender, CSI: Crime Scene Investigation, Without a Trace,* and *Law & Order: Special Victims Unit.*

Andy Botwin, from Zhlubby to Rebbe

A Conversation with Costume Designer

amy STOFSKY

Andy Botwin, Agrestic's sexiest, most charming schnorrer, turns up in Nancy's kitchen in classic T-shirt-wearing slacker form. Costume Designer Amy Stofsky reveals how she upgraded him from a zhlub to a reb-in-training with the help of a top male designer.

Andy loves his T-shirts and cargo pants, but you dress him up quite nicely for rabbinical school in the second season.

Yeah, I took Justin up a notch or two to make Andy look a little more like a man and less like a seventeen-year-old, and then put Hunter [Parrish] in what Justin was wearing the previous season.

Andy wears a black vest, which would seem to be an homage to the ultra-Orthodox.

There was something about the combination of the vest and the white shirt that looked like a contemporary guy's version of a rabbinical student. Hasidic men traditionally wear black three-piece suits. I liked putting Justin in vests. He wore a Star of David once, and I even did *tzitzit* for him, which I think he also wore once. The funny thing is, all of his clothes were John Varvatos—very tailored. The point was ultimately to make him into the heartthrob that he is [*laughs*]. Justin is really the cheerleader of the bunch. He's beautiful—I love him [*laughs*].

SILAS

Nancy Botwin's Kif and Kin:
The Older Son

I f there was one piece of advice Nancy Botwin should have taken from fellow PTA mom Celia Hodes, it was encouraging her sons to discuss Judah's death (see "Nancy Botwin's Kif and Kin: The Dead Husband: Judah Botwin"). At least Shane is dealing with the loss by going to grief counseling and acting weird. But Silas isn't seeing a shrink and Nancy flinches at the mere threat of talking about it with her boys, so he has little choice but to sublimate his anguish and seek solace and distraction from his girlfriends. In the months after his father dies, Silas's attention is pleasantly consumed by the promise of losing his virginity to his first love, Quinn Hodes (see "Celia Hodes's Kif and Kin: The Older Daughter: Quinn Hodes"), the coltish, sexually experienced girl next

BOTWIN

door. But once Quinn's overly watchful mother, Celia, gets wind of their plan from scouring her daughter's diary, she goes on a mission to stop them from ever having sex, and attempts to enlist the help of Nancy. Quinn catches on to Celia's plan and pays her mother halfhearted lip service, but when she's shipped off to a Mexican boarding school just days after she and Silas are caught *in flagrante delicto* by Nancy in the middle of a school day, Silas becomes convinced that Nancy has sold them out. "She just took off without even bothering to say good-bye," cries Silas to his mother. "That's my whole fucking life. People just go away" ("Free Goat").

Not content to be alone, Silas seeks out Megan Beals (see "Silas Botwin's Special Bud: Megan Beals") at a party to see if she lives up to her reputation as a master of the oral arts. He is surprised to find that there is much more than meets the mouth of "the deaf girl on Dewey Street who gave fellatio to Dennis Kling" ("You Can't Miss the Bear"). Silas falls head over heels in love with Megan, who is smart, sassy, and absolutely sexy, and whose generosity with her family lends him the emotional support he lacks at the Botwin household. Even Uncle Andy finds her appealing—he has cybersex with her under the guise of helping Silas move things to the next physical level. It's enough to keep Silas from ever wanting to spend time with his family, especially as he feels himself slowly losing his grip on the reins of his temper. So when Shane filches his Zippo lighter—his one tactile emblem of his father's memory—only to see it confiscated by Principal Dodge (played by David Doty) as punishment for creating a burning bush at school, Silas punches out his younger brother and then flees in terror to the Bealses' house. Nancy gets in her car to look for him and spies Silas through their living room window, being consoled by Megan and her parents—a job she knows she should be doing, if only she wasn't feeling so bereft and lost herself.

It becomes increasingly difficult for Silas to contain his resentment toward his mother and his anger over losing Judah when he becomes cognizant of his mother's new source of income, a moment Nancy has been dreading. She initially denies being a dealer when he confronts her about it. "I live here too, Mom. Or haven't you noticed because you've been so busy with your business? I'm not an idiot. . . . I don't blame you for what you do. You're doing what you need to, I guess. Let's just stay out of each other's way," he says to Nancy ("The Godmother").

Nancy believes Andy has divulged the information. "Silas just informed me that I have no parental rights anymore because I'm a drug dealer. How the fuck did he find out?" she pointedly asks her brother-in-law. "How the fuck did you think he wouldn't, Weedy McWeedWeed?" asks Andy. "He's not mad at you for selling drugs. He's mad at you for lying to him" ("The Godmother"). Home life intensifies further when Silas insistently refers to her by her first name. "Stop calling me Nancy," she scolds. "My name is Mom. Or Mommy Dearest" ("Corn Snake").

When Megan gets an early acceptance to Princeton, Silas becomes terrified about the future of his connection to his surrogate family. The news sends him into a tailspin. Refusing to share Megan's excitement, he tells her, "I can't get into Princeton. I'm not deaf" ("Cooking with Jesus"). After a brief breakup, he pleads with her to get back together. "I fucking miss you. If we only have a few months together, I want to make them count" ("Last Tango in Agrestic"). Desperate to hold on to his relationship with Megan and her parents,

Silas intentionally impregnates his unsuspecting girlfriend, but the plan backfires; rather than becoming forever bonded to the family, he is permanently cast out. Nancy longs to comfort her heartsick, bloodied son, and is furious with Mr. Beals for returning Silas to her like damaged goods after he punched Silas in the face. Suddenly awash in grief—for his father, Megan, the Beals family, the aborted pregnancy, and the life he used to have—Silas feels completely unmoored.

Now that Silas is home, he spends most days hiding behind the locked door of his room, wearing noise-canceling headphones, shutting everybody out. He yearns to be close to Nancy but he doesn't know how to reach out to such an emotionally remote person, no matter how hard she tries to convey her love. As far as Silas can tell, the only way to be in her sphere is to join the family business, but Nancy is determined to keep him out. He becomes frightened of losing his mother when he learns that her new "boyfriend," Peter, is a DEA agent. "What happens when he breaks up with you?" Silas asks Nancy. "Or do you think you're so great that will never happen?" ("Bash"). Finding out that Peter is in fact her husband and can't testify against her does nothing to allay his fears or ease his temper. Equally menacing is the aggressive antidrug campaign launched by Nancy's erstwhile friend and the newly elected city councilperson, Celia Hodes. She has surveillance cameras installed all over Agrestic. Silas decides to run his own one-man clandestine renegade campaign, dismantling the cameras, taking down the signs, and even stealing the Sober the Sasquatch mascot costume. In a horrific twist of fate, he makes a grievous miscalculation when he decides to ratchet up his negotiating tactics by taking the last MILF Weed harvest and holding it ransom in exchange for gaining entry into Nancy's secret world. Not only does this put him in jeopardy of being thrown in the slammer, as Celia tracks him down with a cop in tow, but he unwittingly puts his mother's life in the gravest danger imaginable, stranding her in a room filled with armed and dangerous gangsters looking for their payday.

Megan Beals,
played by Shoshannah Stern

Because Megan is known around Agrestic as "the deaf girl on Dewey Street who gave fellatio to Dennis Kling" ("You Can't Miss the Bear"), Silas seeks her out at a party for the Kling treatment. Instead, she sprays his dick with blue paint. Her sassy nature bewitches him, and Silas quickly discovers that her reputation belies her intelligence, sensitivity, and depth of character. A year older than Silas, the sexy, surly, and frequently forgiving Megan becomes the love of his life, in no small part because she and her family provide him with the support and loving attention he needs in the wake of his father's death, which he can't get from his own family. But she becomes heartbroken when Silas can't bring himself to share in the joy of her early acceptance to Princeton University because of his fear of losing her. After a brief breakup, they resolve to get back together until she goes off to college. Unbeknownst to her, however, he intentionally gets her pregnant to keep her in Agrestic. But her parents won't let anything stop her from pursuing her dream of getting an Ivy League education; they have her end her pregnancy, and they kick a devastated Silas to the curb.

An alumna of Gallaudet University, SHOSHANNAH STERN was born into a fourth-generation deaf family. Stern currently appears in the hit series *Jericho*, and enjoyed a recurring role in the series *Threat Matrix* that was specifically written for her after the director and producers saw her work on an episode of *The Division*.

HASHING IT OUT WITH ...
HUNTER PARRISH

What were your first impressions of Silas?

The first time I read him, I liked the truth behind the relationship with Quinn Hodes [played by Haley Hudson], because it was all about Quinn at that moment. It was exciting to be in love with someone who was in love with me. There was this great scene that was actually cut, where we were in the back of this ballpark making out, and I was pressuring her to have sex, because I hadn't done it yet. I was like, "C'mon, what's the problem? Why can't we just go in the car and have sex? I have my mom's keys." I was bummed it was cut; it was definitely my favorite scene in the pilot because there was so much of Silas in it and that was what really drew me to the role.

His father, Judah, died at a crucial juncture in his life. Only Silas's younger brother, Shane, is able to express his grief.

Alexander can say a line like "I got rage in me" and make it work [*laughs*]. If I had been given that line, I would have never known what to do with it. The only time we see Silas express his grief is when he punches Shane in the face after he steals Dad's lighter from Silas's drawer. He's grasping on to every last bit of his dad that he can, and not finding it in anything but a tactile object. He loves Shane, and wants to be the big brother for him, but since we don't talk about Dad's death at home, Silas knew he needed to find understanding elsewhere, so he flees to Megan's family. I think that was one of his biggest moments, because Silas needed to release everything that he'd been holding within himself.

Do you think Andy is a good father figure for Silas and Shane, subversive though he is?

He definitely is for Shane. I think if Andy wasn't there, Silas would have a lot more issues, because without him, he would have no one. Before Silas broke up with Megan he got a lot from Megan's dad, but now, whether he wants to admit it or not, he's leaning on Andy a lot more. When he tells Andy that Megan's going to Princeton, Andy tells him to get a van, and Silas listens to his advice, and they really bond because he's there to give him advice when Mom isn't there. And they bond again when they're lying in the pool feeling jilted by Nancy because they both feel that Nancy is screwing them over. They don't know who she is anymore and she's not letting either of them be a part of the business.

Silas has had an incredibly difficult journey, especially in season two, after he intentionally gets Megan pregnant to keep her from going away to Princeton. As Silas, you have to say some very offensive things in those moments to Shoshannah Stern, who plays Megan, and who is deaf in real life. What was that like for you?

I'm best friends with Shoshannah, so she knows the difference between me and Silas, and knows I would never say things like that. We're comfortable talking about her being deaf. But I did ask her, "Does this offend you?" And she said, "Yeah, a little." I didn't expect her to say that. I thought for sure she'd say, "Whatever, it's just a show." To be honest, it made me make it more offensive because I wanted to see how she'd react; if she was offended just by reading it, then I needed to go big. Shoshannah and I love acting together, so the more conflict I can put in there, the more we have to go on. I think Silas had no idea how hurtful his words were because he loves her. When you're angry, you think of the most hurtful thing to say just to get back at the person. Throughout the series, we'd made jokes about her character being deaf—she's first introduced as "the deaf girl on Dewey Street who gave fellatio to Dennis Kling." I always worried about what Shoshannah thought, but she embraced it, used it, and always found the comedy. She's such a beautiful person and a fantastic actress. And through being friends, I've learned so much about the deaf community.

Do you relate to Silas?

Yeah. About sixty percent of Silas is like me. I'm nineteen [*laughs*] and I'm looking at the sixteen-year-old that I'm playing, and he's going through a lot of the same things that I'm going through, at least in the first season, because the world is opening up for him. I've never smoked pot and I am not a promiscuous person [*laughs*], but I think I understand him being lost and being in pain and how he feels it. Toward the end of the second season, I identify with his love and desire to protect his mother and show her that he loves her—his love is strangely expressed, but it's there. You struggle with proving yourself to your mom, trying to tell her "I do know," or "I can say that I know this."

As a viewer of the show, are there scenes that particularly resonate with you?

The one where Nancy is watching the film footage of herself with Judah. Every time I watch [that scene]—and I'll watch it three or four times in a row—I cry. I can't take my eyes off of her. She's watching the video, and her hands are wrapped around her knees, and at one point, she puts her hand up to her mouth and it takes away everything except her eyes and that's all that needs to be there.

Who are some of your favorite characters?

I hated Andy last year, but I love him now. There are so many aspects to Andy that went *ka-boom* and spread all over. That masturbation monologue he gave—how brilliant was that? [*Laughs*] He had so much incredible material to play with. I also really like Pam Gruber [played by Becky Thyre] [*laughs*]. That "be my friend" scene, oh my God—when Celia was like, "Selfish, selfish, selfish"—I just cried when she said that, and then when she leans up against the wall and says to Nancy, "Talk to me. Can't you just talk to me?" Elizabeth was so brilliant in that scene. What I love about Jenji is that there is so much we want to do or say to people, like everyone does with Nancy, and there's that one person who can do it, and Celia's that person. The mix of characters in this show is the driving force of this whole catastrophe. I'm really impressed by the changes between season one and season two, with Pam and Isabel. Allie Grant rocks. When Celia sprains her groin after that workout, and is lying on the ground, and Isabel is clapping her hands, and says, "All right, c'mon! We're not here to sit around," it is clear that, as much as she hates her, Isabel's becoming Celia—how could she not? She lives with it. Every single character has their own story line twist and something interesting to do. I also love Renée Victor. Lupita has two of my favorite lines, one that she says to Nancy: "I think you have too much love and trust for me to ever let me go." [*Laughs*] My other is from the second season, when she says to Celia after Celia's car accident with another maid, "I don't know, we just call each other 'maid friend.'" Renée and I have made up a whole subplot twist where we are going to have a secret affair pretty soon [*laughs*]. By far, though, my favorite character is Nancy—I am just so infatuated with the on-screen charisma that is there.

What's it like having Mary-Louise as your fictional mother?

When I first met her, I was young and we argued about a lot of things. During the pilot I just wanted to make friends with people because I thought it meant we'd act well together. If I don't get along with people, I have trouble focusing on my words and character and the point of what I'm doing because I'll be worrying about what they're thinking. And I was really scared of her [*laughs*]. We didn't have a lot of scenes together in the first season, so I got to learn about myself before I had to face Mary-Louise. In the second season, we had to face each other a lot, and with every scene we did, I learned something. I could go on and on about how closely I watch her. We talk a lot. She's there for me and I feel lucky that, despite everything we argued about during the pilot [*laughs*], I'm able to talk to someone that I respect so much, about things that I can't talk to anyone else about.

HUNTER PARRISH has guest starred in the television series *CSI: Crime Scene Investigation*, *Summerland*, *Close to Home*, *Skater Boys*, and *Campus Ladies*. He appears in the films *Freedom Writers* with Hilary Swank, *Down in the Valley* with Edward Norton, and *Steal Me*, which premiered at Sundance in 2007 in the American Spectrum category and earned Parrish the Method Fest award in the best actor category for his performance. He has also had roles in the Barry Sonnenfeld movie *RV* with Robin Williams, and *Sleepover*.

THE DOPE ON . . .

Nancy Botwin's Kif and Kin: The Younger Son

SHANE

BOTWIN

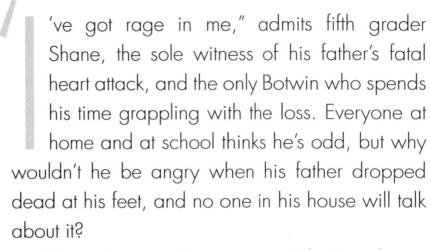

"'ve got rage in me," admits fifth grader Shane, the sole witness of his father's fatal heart attack, and the only Botwin who spends his time grappling with the loss. Everyone at home and at school thinks he's odd, but why wouldn't he be angry when his father dropped dead at his feet, and no one in his house will talk about it?

When Shane isn't spying on Silas's make-out sessions with his girlfriend, he's hiding up in the rafters, where he sits for hours watching old home videos of Judah (see "Nancy Botwin's Kif and Kin: The Dead Husband: Judah Botwin"), rewinding the parts where his father tells him, "To me you're the best. The unbelievable, amazing Shane Botwin" ("Free Goat"). But the kids at school just think he's "Strange" Botwin. His Hurricanes teammates, led by star player Devon Rensler (played by Adam Taylor Gordon), intentionally kick him during the soccer matches—the sight of Shane licking his own blood is a perfect opportunity to taunt him even more—and call him Orphan Boy. Shane might be scared of Devon and his friends, but he's a fearless avenger the next day at school, when, dressed in camouflage, he leaps out of a tree, carrying a water Uzi, pummeling them with sprays of pink paint. "I think pink's really your color, you fuckwad!" ("You Can't Miss the Bear").

The paint gun incident turns out to be the first of many times Nancy is summoned to the office of Principal Dodge (played by David Doty) to discuss Shane's increasingly violent behavior. Shane is finally brought in to see Dr. Schloss, the school psychologist (played by Amy Aquino), who is concerned about his violent gangsta rap: "My name is Shane / I bring in the pain / Up from the streets of Agrestic / Bitch you don't want to sweat this / I'll cap any motherfucker / You don't wanna test this, beeyotch." Shane explains to Dr. Schloss, "I'm just venting . . . [against] a bunch of bitch-ass white boys" ("'Lude Awakening"). Being self-aware—and undergoing psychotherapy—earns Shane a pass out of Schloss's office. He attracts Nancy's attention when he shoots a roaming mountain lion with a BB gun, which she takes away from him, and brings her to the negotiating table with his homemade

terrorist video, which shows him beheading Doug Wilson's daughter. Shane knows he has his mother's love, but the challenge is getting her to notice him these days.

The unannounced arrival of Uncle Andy may not be welcome in his mother's eyes, but Shane couldn't be more overjoyed, especially since Silas is all-consumed with Megan (see "Silas Botwin's Special Bud: Megan Beals"), Nancy is becoming increasingly distracted by her mysterious errands, and Lupita has her hands full cleaning up after all of them. Uncle Andy's judgment is not usually sound—he gets Shane suspended for helping him sell "Chris Died for Your Sins" T-shirts at school—but he does his best to troubleshoot Shane's

problems, and, most important, spend quality time with him. Uncle Andy tells the best gross jokes as he teaches him and his friend Max Dodd (played by Forrest Landis) how to cook osso bucco and orders the teacher's edition of Shane's science textbook to help him cheat on his tests, advising him to miss a couple of answers so that his test score seems realistic. Uncle Andy even comes to the rescue when Shane gets in trouble for "gumming up" the plumbing with "jerk socks" ("Last Tango in Agrestic"). Nancy's attempts at talking to Shane about puberty and jerking off freak them both out, so she farms out the job to her brother-in-law. Who better to teach Shane about his changing body than the master . . . bator? Shane might not be able to make sense of half of what he's saying—"lubricated flak catchers," "slip the peel over your Randy Johnson and start pitching," "work on your control now, while you're a solo artist, and you'll be playing some long happy duets in the future" ("Last Tango in Agrestic")—but when Uncle Andy tosses him a banana, he's only too eager to figure it out in the privacy of his bedroom. And when he tells his uncle that the boys at school are reaming him for being a hand job virgin, Andy has a quick fix: He whisks him off to a massage parlor, where a nice lady named Jade gives him the professional treatment. But what happens in the massage parlor should remain in the massage parlor, lest Nancy find out.

Since entering the fifth grade, Shane's violent outbursts have subsided, though he is still struggling with his status as an outcast. He develops a huge crush on the beautiful brace-faced Gretchen (see "Shane Botwin's Special Bud: Gretchen"), but can't quite find the right approach. He learns the hard way that staring at her in class and kicking her in the leg in the hallway aren't going to endear him to her. His plan to join the debate team is ruined by the coach, Mr. Albin (played by Remy Auberjonois), who has them face off on the electoral college versus popular vote. Gretchen doesn't even get the chance to weigh in, because Shane has the advantage of arguing in favor of the popular vote. The answer to him is simple: "George W. Bush." Dejected, he tells his mother he is going to resign

from the debate team. Nancy tries to comfort him by sharing the story of her own awkward beginnings with Judah. But he has decidedly put his grief behind him, even if she hasn't dealt with her anguish. "I don't want to talk about [Gretchen] to you. . . . Why do you always have to bring up Dad?" ("Must Find Toes").

Shane finally wins Gretchen's heart, and the respect of his peers, when he calls newly elected councilwoman Celia Hodes on her hypocrisy during her patronizing antidrug speech. He tells her, "I think you're turning Agrestic into a police state! I've seen you drunk at my house. Not like the drunken homeless penguins in the ghetto, but I've definitely seen you drunk. And isn't being drunk just like being on drugs? Isn't alcohol a drug? You do drugs!" ("MILF Money"). Finally he is able to trade in his Strange Botwin reputation for one more akin to Norma Rae, and as his classmates celebrate his smart-alecky courage and elect him as their class speaker for graduation, delivering Agrestic Elementary's most profane speech in the school's history—"There are motherfucking snakes on this motherfucking plane!" ("Pittsburgh")—Gretchen invites him to become her boyfriend. Their relationship is doomed, however, when Uncle Andy's ex-girlfriend Kat (see "Andy Botwin's Special Buds: Kat") lands on the Botwins' doorstep. Shane is immediately taken with her . . . before he will be taken *by* her after his graduation party, as she flees from an Inuit bounty hunter named Abumchuk (played by Robert Allen Mukes) and whisks him off to Paraguay.

Shane enjoys the vindication of becoming the most popular kid in school, but his real motivation for derailing Celia's presentation is to protect his mother. He suspects that she's dealing drugs, though no one has ever told him. Nothing frightens him more than the thought of Nancy's getting busted and his losing another parent, a possibility made all the more real when he notices that her "boyfriend," Peter Scottson, is wearing a DEA jacket. When Nancy tells the family they might be relocating, he is determined to clear the air, once and for all. "You *are* a drug dealer," he says. "Yes, Shane. I grow and sell marijuana," says Nancy. "It's organic. It's therapeutic. It's of the earth. Like tomatoes." Shane is as incredulous as he is terrified. "Yeah. Like tomatoes" ("Yeah. Like Tomatoes").

Shane Botwin's Special Bud

Gretchen,
played by Eden Sher

Sulky, tall, metal-mouthed Gretchen is a fellow fifth grader who becomes the object of Shane's infatuation—and eventually his first girlfriend. Wordless stares from "Strange" Botwin do not endear him to her, and neither does the random hard kick in her shin in front of her locker. Any hope of changing his luck appears doomed when Shane joins the debate team in an effort to get to know her because their coach, Mr. Albin, pits them against each other to face off on the topic of the electoral college versus popular vote: Shane swiftly if inadvertently shuts her down with the perfect three-word argument: "George W. Bush." But Gretchen reconsiders her feelings for Shane when he causes a riot during an antidrug speech given by newly elected councilwoman Celia Hodes, after he tells her he thinks she is turning Agrestic into a police state and calls her on her hypocrisy by announcing to the class that he has seen her drunk at his house. Now that he's the fifth grade's class hero, Gretchen agrees to be his girlfriend, on the condition that they don't kiss until her braces come off and "that won't be for a while. Like maybe even a year" ("Bash"). Shane is happy to oblige her any which way—that is, until Uncle Andy's wild ex-girlfriend, Kat, shows up at their doorstep. Gretchen is certain that Kat wants in on her action, but she's not going to give up her little man so easily. Their middle school graduation party decides the fate of the relationship for them when a love-struck Shane is kidnapped by Kat, and a dejected Gretchen declares the relationship officially over.

EDEN SHER has guest starred on *The O.C.* and had a recurring role on *Sons and Daughters*.

HASHING IT OUT WITH...
aLEXaNDER GOULD

What did you think of Shane when you went to the *Weeds* audition?

I really didn't want to do the audition because there was a little bit of bad language and I wasn't very comfortable with saying those things. My mom said, "I think it's really good for you. Just deal with it and pretend you're saying something completely different. I know it's a bad word, but it's just a bad word." So I did the audition, and once I started, I thought it was a great role, and easy for me to play. The bad language, which had progressed a little bit—you know, I kept saying bad language throughout the season and everything—it was all right. I just would go away from it. I'm not like that in real life at all.

How old were you when the pilot was shot?

I think I'd just turned ten.

Have you ever met anyone like Shane before?

Sort of. He likes high places. I also love high places. You saw him in the first season when he broke his arm? I have a loft bed, and I always like going up, climbing up ladders and going on rooftops and that kind of thing. But I don't use foul language at all or anything like that.

How would you describe him?

Shane is really smart. He's probably almost on genius level but he doesn't ever show it. He tries to find his way. He's devastated by his father's death. And he always wants to fit in and never quite makes it—well, except at the end of the season. Shane definitely changes from season one to two. In school he's gotten a lot more popular. He's pretty much the same guy but he's a lot more confident. And he knows more than any twelve-year-old boy should know.

Are there scenes that best convey who Shane is?

There are three of them, I think: The scene where Shane is telling off Celia in the classroom during her antidrug talk. Also, I think when he gives his speech at the graduation in "Pittsburgh." And I think in the episode where Shane finally finds out that Nancy is a drug dealer.

Do you like his relationship with Uncle Andy?

I do. Justin [Kirk] is also really nice. It's fun, I guess. I think he [Andy] tries to be good to Shane and Silas, but he usually ends up doing it in the completely wrong way—nasty—but that's the only way he knows.

Is Uncle Andy one of your favorite characters?

Yeah. He's just a loser, but a loser that you like. I also thought Kat was a really neat character. It was a crazy new twist and Zooey Deschanel was great to work with.

Being a member of the Botwin family must be fun.

Everyone in that family is really crazy. Uncle Andy could be a great chef. He makes all of these wonderful meals, but he's a loser who smokes pot and all of that. Silas is also really smart but he never shows it. He's pretty cool, I guess. Nancy doesn't know what to do most of the time. Obviously she's dealing pot, and she's in with people she probably shouldn't be in with, but she's found a way to get by and still have money and everything.

What's it like to work with Mary-Louise?

She's given me a lot of good tips on acting and she's really nice to me. She doesn't talk to me much, but when she does, she seems to really like me a lot.

I hear Hunter Parrish organized a really cool scavenger hunt on the set for your birthday. You two must have become really close.

Yeah, we've really become good friends—almost like brothers in real life.

What is your favorite scene?

The scene where I was up on top of the rafters watching the camera. That was fun to do. Also when I was up in the tree and I jumped down on those kids.

What do you like to do when you're not acting?

I like to swim and play golf and video games. I have a PSP and a Nintendo DS. I have a lot of video games, too many to name, but my favorite one for my PSP is "Untold Legends." It's pretty much my favorite game out of all of them.

What do you think is going to happen to Shane and his family?

I think it would be really fun to go work in Mexico for a week. Or even Pittsburgh. That'd be interesting. I think Silas is going to wind up going to jail—something crazy is going to happen with that. I also think something is going to happen with Shane and Kat, where Kat gets put in jail. And then Kat and Silas break out together and try to make their way to Paraguay or something.

ALEXANDER GOULD began his acting career at age two with his first speaking role. Since then he has had a successful career on the big and small screens, including providing the voice of Nemo in the hit animated feature *Finding Nemo*. His other feature work includes *Wheelmen* and the suspense thriller *They*. Gould has guest starred on such critically acclaimed series as *Ally McBeal*, *Malcolm in the Middle*, *7th Heaven*, *Family Law*, and *Even Stevens*. Most recently he costarred in the series *Boomtown* and was seen in the television movies *The Day the World Ended* and *The Point of Origin*. His latest voice work can be heard in the 2006 *Bambi II*, the sequel to the much loved Disney classic.

Nancy Botwin's Kif and Kin:
The Dead Husband

Judah Botwin
played by Jeffrey Dean Morgan

Judah is Andy's older brother, Nancy's husband, and the father of Silas and Shane. Dead of a heart attack at forty, Judah and his innumerable virtues emerge near-mythic through the stories related by those who love him, and in home movies watched by Nancy, and by Shane, who was jogging with him when he died. Since his death, Judah's grief-stricken family commemorates his birthday annually with an evening devoted to his favorite things: a screening of the original Willy Wonka & the Chocolate Factory, a chicken parmigiana dinner, and a piñata filled with Almond Joy candy bars. According to Andy, Judah met Nancy during his tortured-artist phase, when he hired her to dance in his performance art piece, "Feet Me in St. Louis" ("Bash"). "But he was always broke, and it wasn't his true nature, and your mom wanted kids, so he took his engineering degree, got a 'real' job, and moved to suburbia," Andy tells Silas. "He was the golden child to my black sheep. Did everything right. A mother's dream. Hardworking, athletic, ambitious" ("Bash"). Nancy believes Judah was the better parent, and in a moment of frustration with Silas, blurts out, "The wrong parent died!" ("Bash"). Nancy realizes just how much she is still contending with the loss when Shane saturates himself in Judah's cologne to impress a girl, and the scent conjures memories for Nancy of a young Budweiser-swilling, goatee-sprouting Judah, who slept on a futon and hit on her roommate before the two of them would get to know one another and fall in love. Though we see less and less of Judah, the presence of his absence is as palpable as ever in the Botwin home.

JEFFREY DEAN MORGAN is a prolific television actor. He has had recurring roles most recently on *Grey's Anatomy* and *Supernatural*, and has also guest starred on *Monk*, *CSI: Crime Scene Investigation*, *Tru Calling*, *The O.C.*, *JAG*, and *The Division*, among many other television series.

LUPITa

t may be a dubious honor, but Nancy counts Lupita, the Botwins' sassy housekeeper, among her family members. The Botwins have always had a more liberal parenting approach than Lupita, but the single mother from El Salvador, who is putting her daughter through court-reporting school, hasn't been hired to judge the family or wipe down their moral slates; she's there for domestic upkeep. Since "Mr. Judah" (see "Nancy Botwin's Kif and Kin: The Dead Husband: Judah Botwin") died, however, the household rules, such as they are, appear to be more lax than usual. Silas can usually be found in his room having sex with his girlfriend—first Quinn Hodes (see "Celia Hodes's Kif and Kin: The Older Daughter: Quinn Hodes"), then Megan Beals (see "Silas Botwin's Special Bud:

Megan Beals"). Shane is either hanging from the rafters watching old videos of his dad, making terrorist videos of his own, or spying on his brother's sexploits. Nancy isn't always keeping up with the bills and tends to disappear for hours at a time even though she is supposedly unemployed and single. And worst of all, Judah's younger, pothead brother, Andy, moves in unannounced and makes a mess of everything he touches. And most often he's touching himself.

Though she does not have full command of English, Lupita's keen intuition and sardonic wit cross the language barrier, which serves her well as the fly on the wall in this crazy household. Lupita has no desire to ask about the blue paint she scrubs from the crotch of Silas's pants or the man-sauce-filled socks that Shane is stuffing in the pipes. Andy and Doug's impromptu pot, porn, and perineum festival disgusts her, but she settles their argument over the name of "the thing between the dick and the asshole" without flinching or missing a beat: "The coffee table" ("'Lude Awakening"). She senses that Nancy is up to something strange when the butter she's using looks and smells weird. Nancy claims that it's sage. Lupita knows better. "Obviously menopause has altered your sense of smell," Nancy tells her. "I no smell with my coochie," Lupita quips ("Good Shit Lollipop").

But Lupita isn't going to push Nancy. If anything, she is Nancy's apologist and

defender against everything that threatens her and the family, from the circulating gossip about her new source of income, to the cryptic messages left for Nancy by Alejandro Rivera, Agrestic's main purveyor of shwag (see "Nancy Botwin's Contact Highs: The Head of Distribution: Alejandro Rivera"). Until Lupita sees the proof with her own eyes, she refuses to believe the rumors. That's not to say she won't scour the house in pursuit of evidence, but as she searches every drawer, box, and closet while Nancy is out of the house, Lupita hopes against hope that she won't find so much as a stem.

So discovering Nancy's stash isn't so much of a bust as it is a rude awakening.

But it's one that Lupita knows how to use to her advantage. She shows her "missus" the greenery, and announces she wants a raise. "Maybe you have too much love and TRUST for me to ever let me go," she gently taunts Nancy ("Corn Snake"). And while Lupita is happy to help Nancy shield Shane from learning about the business, she also sees this potent new information as an opportunity to lighten her workload—Nancy isn't exactly in a bargaining position, after all. With Nancy spending more time at the grow house and being less of a presence at home with the boys, though, Lupita and Andy step up to the plate and parent the kids.

Lupita picks up on the increasing danger in Nancy's life, but she's too terrified to ask any questions. Finally Nancy approaches her, and without divulging any details, gives Lupita instructions on what to do in case of a dire emergency. "Nothing [is gonna happen]. But if something did, the kids go to my sister, Jill. *Not* Andy." Lupita has never been more certain of her familial connection to the Botwins. "Okay," she says, stunned. "Now I go light a candle" ("Pittsburgh").

HASHING IT OUT WITH . . .
Renée VICTOR

Nancy's housekeeper, Lupita, is one of the funniest, most droll characters on the series. What do you think of her?

I love her sarcasm. When Lupita is searching the house for evidence that Nancy's dealing, and little Shane asks her, "Are you stealing from us again?" she is standing there with a menorah, and comes back at him with, "*Jes*. My family needs a menorah." Or after Celia's car accident, when she asks Lupita if the woman is one of her "maid friends," and Celia says, "Do you know her? What's her name?" Lupita says, "Oh, we just call each other 'maid friend.'" There are people who lack education or money, but they aren't self-conscious or frightened. I'm guessing she is probably an illegal immigrant from El Salvador, working as a maid because she doesn't have a command of the language and she isn't educated. But I've met people like her, who are gracious, and assertive, and comfortable wherever they are because they are comfortable in their own skin. It would be very easy for her to discuss anything with Nancy and Doug and Celia.

Did you invent a back story for Lupita?

Yes. I saw that the Botwin household was very informal, because, in the pilot, a teenage boy walks past me and takes his girlfriend right to his bedroom. That would never happen in Lupita's home, or in my culture—my mother is Hispanic, and my father is Italian. I gathered from the pilot that theirs was not an ordinary home, and those boys aren't typical of America's suburbs, so therefore they would not have the typical maid, either. Nancy probably interviewed several women, and figured she couldn't have a holier-than-thou woman in her home, so she picked the assertive, open one. Lupita might speak up, but she's not going to impose her moral code on the family. In the second episode, Lupita reveals she has an ex-husband and a boyfriend, so she hasn't exactly kept her knickers on all the time, either.

But she'll never abandon Nancy or those kids. She doesn't approve of what Nancy is doing, but she's not going to leave. She loves those boys. She's not crazy about Andy [*laughs*], but she figures if he's getting away with murder, I'm getting away with a little bit too.

Lupita is the fly on the wall of the Botwin family household, witnessing more than she would ever want to of the lives of Andy, teenage Silas, pubescent Shane, and drug-dealing Nancy. What was the most challenging scene for you?

The one where I had to tell Nancy that the little boy was whacking off and he left the "man sauce" in socks, while the older boy used T-shirts, and I said, "Too bad Mr. Judah isn't here now that the little one started whacking." I'm talking about masturbation, y'know? [*Laughs*] The show has a lot of pain, and a lot of humor. I commend the writers because the writing is so magnificent.

What's it like to be a part of the Botwin household?

It's heaven. I adore Mary-Louise—I'd admired her for so long as an actress. The thing that moves me the most about her is her dedication as a mother. That baby is her life. And at the same time, she doesn't overdo it, just like her work. She doesn't overdo anything and it's so powerful. I really love that about her. And my Hunter—I always tease him and say, "You know, they're writing an episode where I seduce you?" [*Laughs.*] It's hard for me to keep my hands off of that little Alex. I just want to take his face and squeeze it and tell his mother that he's coming home with me. I know that I can't because he's right at that age when that sort of thing embarrasses boys, so I remind myself not to do it. But I'm very demonstrative and affectionate—I'm the same way with my daughters. That Alex is a good kid and such a talented little actor. And Justin Kirk is absolutely brilliant—I love him. He's one of the best actors around. Craig Zisk is a wonderful director and he gives his actors freedom. I've actually worked with both of the Zisk brothers—I love those boys. Craig encourages everyone and gets the best out of everyone. This is probably the first ensemble group of actors and writers and producers and directors that I've worked with where no one has an attitude. But it all starts at the top, darling, and it trickles on down. When my daughter met Jenji, she said, "Mom, you just get some good vibes from her."

Before becoming an actress, you used to be a singer and a choreographer. Do you still do either of these things?

I still teach dancing, and occasionally I'll do singing gigs, though not too often because I can't be up until past midnight and then be up so early in the morning. It has taken its toll on my voice, too. I've done choreography for Gena Rowlands, I've taught Andy Garcia, I've worked with Robert Duvall. I used to be a professional dancer in Vegas, which led me to my singing career, and then I studied to become an actress. I think it would be fun if maybe someday Lupita sings a little bit, or teaches Shane how to do the cha-cha.

RENÉE VICTOR worked as a professional choreographer, singer, and dancer before she began her acting career in television and film nearly twenty-five years ago. She had a recurring role on *ER* and appeared in Robert Duvall's feature film *Assassination Tango*.

THE DOPE on . . .

PETER

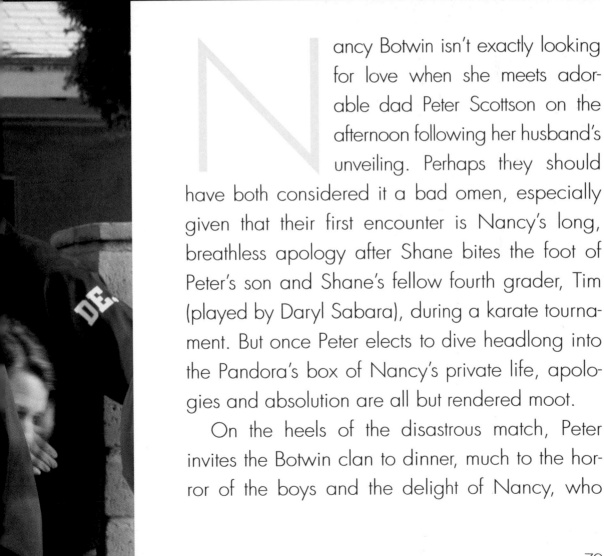

SCOTTSON

Nancy Botwin isn't exactly looking for love when she meets adorable dad Peter Scottson on the afternoon following her husband's unveiling. Perhaps they should have both considered it a bad omen, especially given that their first encounter is Nancy's long, breathless apology after Shane bites the foot of Peter's son and Shane's fellow fourth grader, Tim (played by Daryl Sabara), during a karate tournament. But once Peter elects to dive headlong into the Pandora's box of Nancy's private life, apologies and absolution are all but rendered moot.

On the heels of the disastrous match, Peter invites the Botwin clan to dinner, much to the horror of the boys and the delight of Nancy, who

appears to be as drawn to him as he is rapt by her. And with every glass of wine she guzzles—one, it seems, to match each of Shane's pointedly candid, discomfort-inducing questions—she becomes endearingly loopier and sexier, until she finally interrupts her own rambling monologue to kiss him. Could Nancy be the antidote to his recent heartbreaking divorce from the wife who cheated on him? Not if she keeps pulling back the way she does in the middle of their first liplock. If only he'd realize she's trying to protect him. But he persists in his pursuit, making himself readily available, and he believes it pays off. Peter and Nancy talk on the phone late at night, and finally she gives in and turns up at his door for an impromptu late-night date. No sooner do they enjoy a passionate night together than Nancy appears to get freaked out by the sight of his gun and his DEA jacket. She tries to end things with him before a relationship begins, telling him, "I'm a widow. And I'm just starting to get back on my feet and I can't get involved with someone who does what you do. . . . I can't get close to you and then lose you. . . . I need to end this now. . . . Please don't call me again" ("Corn Snake"). He recognizes a brush-off when he hears one, especially since he's done a little investigating on Nancy's background. Unfortunately there is no gentle way to disclose this fact to Nancy without terrifying her, judging from her reaction: When he tells Nancy he knows that she's dealing pot, she bolts out of his car with lightning speed and throws up on her front lawn. She is so convinced he is going to arrest her that she is unable to hear his assurances that her dime-bag business is beneath his radar. "Small potatoes," he says. You're a "teeny, tiny fish in a deep and vast narcotic sea." Over dinner, Nancy eyes him suspiciously. "You could be setting me up. . . . What if this is all an act you put on to nail perps?" Peter responds, "Take them to dinner and profess my love? It's how I took down the Santiago brothers" ("Last Tango in Agrestic").

But Peter has his heart set on being with Nancy, and finds a way to make it work for both of them: He whisks her away to Las Vegas, where they marry so that he won't ever be able to testify against her. Though the secret plan is strictly a business arrangement—they aren't living together or informing their respective families, and he gives Nancy the marriage certificate to do with what she will—Peter harbors hopes that the marriage, and Nancy, will eventually turn legit. But Nancy has a different plan in mind: Soon after they marry, she shows Peter a map of a residential cul-de-sac, the site of her new grow house, which, she's just learned, is surrounded by the Northside Armenian Power. "I'm thinking this wasn't one of my vows," Peter tells Nancy angrily ("Mrs. Botwin's Neighborhood"). But he not only signed on for this collusion with Nancy; he eagerly sought it out. In his capacity as an increasingly corrupt DEA agent, he has all of the Armenian grow houses raided, leaving hers to operate in peace—what better wedding present for his new pot-dealer wife than her own neighborhood?

Nancy's increasing commitment to her business demands Peter's compromise of his ethics and jeopardizes his entire livelihood. But he's more than willing to risk everything for her. That is, until she introduces him to her business partner, Conrad Shepard, whose good looks put Peter on edge, causing him to wonder if Nancy's partnership is rooted much deeper than the mother plant Conrad and she share. Perhaps Conrad is right to be mistrustful of him, even though Peter explains, "You don't have to trust me. You trust your partner. Who happens to be my partner. So by the transitive property of partner trust, we trust each other" ("Crush Girl Love Panic").

Once Nancy betrays Peter's confidence by tipping off Heylia James about a planned DEA raid, that transitive property of partner trust starts to crumble. Heylia foils Peter by hosting a Nation of Islam meeting in her home, which casts Peter in a foolish light—he has promised his boss that she would be his ticket to busting U-Turn (see "Nancy Botwin's Obstacle Courses: U-Turn"), the biggest game in West Adams. Peter makes his first demand of Nancy, that she strongly consider legitimizing their marriage and beg out of dealing. But she has no desire to quit now that MILF Weed has emerged as the hottest strain in the region. Conrad begs her to stick it out with Peter, however, in the interest of protecting their business.

Nancy invites Peter over for dinner to officially introduce him to her family, but Silas's contempt for Peter—he hates him for who he is (a DEA agent) and who he isn't (Judah)—dooms the evening. He ultimately incites Peter's temper when he refuses to remove his elbow from the dinner table; Peter reflexively yanks the boy's arm off the table. Nancy is stunned into silence: Hurting one of her kids has always been a deal breaker, but she is determined to yield to "Conrad's plan." She can't stop thinking about what Peter did to Silas, even as they go up to her bedroom and prepare for what becomes the most awkward sexual encounter of their relationship. As she and Peter start to kiss, she asks him, "Why did you . . . do that to his elbow?" ("Mile Deep and a Foot Wide").

The growing chasm between Peter and Nancy is palpable and it's driving him crazy—he senses Nancy has no interest in looking out for anyone but herself. He has to know what she's thinking about him and about Conrad. Moments after leaving Nancy's house, Peter taps in to her phone line and listens in on a conversation, devastated as he hears

her and Conrad referring to him as Agent Wonderbread. Worse yet, Nancy tells Conrad, "I don't want [Peter] ever coming back. . . . I don't love him. And I'm never gonna love him" ("Mile Deep and a Foot Wide"). Enraged and wholly convinced that the two are having an affair, Peter turns up at the grow house the next day, coldcocks Conrad and keeps him pinned to the ground with his foot, and demands Nancy hand him the marriage certificate—their deal is off. But the certificate

is already mailed in. Peter must resort to a brutal Plan B: Nancy and Conrad must sell the last harvest to a single buyer, hand all the money over to Agent Wonderbread, and then "make every effort to ensure that I never see you again. . . . [And] if you'd prefer prison to giving up your payday, I will take you down, and if I go too, serves me right. I put everything on the line for you and you fucked me. I want [Nancy] to live to regret. [Conrad], I regret that you live" ("Yeah. Like Tomatoes"). Conrad negotiates a deal with U-Turn, who agrees to buy the MILF Weed for $300,000. Nancy doesn't know it, but Heylia brokers a deal of her own with Northside Armenian Power drug lord Aram Kesheshian (see "Nancy Botwin's Obstacle Courses: Aram Kesheshian"), who puts out a hit on Peter before he can even see the deal go down.

HASHING IT OUT WITH ...
martin donovan

When Peter is first introduced, he seems like a good enough guy. Do you think falling in love with Nancy is what set him off, or do you imagine he was always prone to corruption?

I imagine he had a propensity toward cutting corners if it needed to happen. I think he starts off being kind of solid—rational and responsible. But he has his issues and becomes more and more ethically compromised. It really took this woman that he loved to push him over the edge; otherwise he probably wouldn't have done anything quite like this. I do think he has an innate tendency to rationalize.

In the postconventional-moralistic world of *Weeds*, drug dealers are the heroes, and the DEA agent is vilified. What has it been like for you to portray someone like Peter Scottson?

I've talked to Mary-Louise about this because I love her so much, but having to feign rage toward her was extremely hard, and it was also hurtful to be around, and to be treated that way by her character. That's maybe where I'm taking my character home? [*Laughs*] This is the fourth time she and I have worked together, and the first time we've done a series together. I think she had lobbied for me to get this role, so it was a great opportunity to work with an old friend. But it got really difficult, because I didn't enjoy playing the dissolution of the relationship between Nancy and Peter as it was coming unglued and getting nasty.

The relationship between Peter and Nancy was tenuous from the beginning because she approached it with caution. But it didn't appear to be dangerous until she learned he's a DEA agent. During a dinner party, when Nancy formally introduces Peter to the family, he reprimands Silas and throws his elbow off of the dinner table, which proves to be the deal breaker for her. What did you make of that moment?

I think Peter did that impulsively. I don't think he was conscious of having crossed a line there. It didn't register, even when Nancy asks, "Why did you do that?" I think he may have even forgotten it happened. People do things that are manifestations of a very deep psychological orientation and they're not aware that they're doing it, and they keep doing it.

What was your favorite scene to do?

The scene where Peter comes to Nancy's door with a bag of oranges the morning after he's listened in on the phone call with Conrad. I thought it was really interesting. I love the way it was written. "I got you some oranges." It's not clear what he's doing, and I don't think he knows what he's doing either. He probably had one idea, like, "I'm going to tell her to go fuck herself," or whatever. I'm sure he had about four different ideas and it changed five times while he was talking to her. That's why that scene was written so brilliantly, because it's really obtuse. She doesn't know what the hell is going on. It was one of the most challenging and fun scenes to do.

What do you think it is about Nancy that made him fall in love with her?

I think she makes him laugh. She's so tangential, and her tangents are fascinating. She'll be talking about one thing and then she ricochets and goes back to something you were talking about a paragraph earlier. I think he fell in love with the way she bounces around, the way her mind works—it's lovely to behold.

Have you ever lived in a place like Agrestic?

I grew up in the suburbs of the San Fernando Valley of L.A., which is not as upscale as Agrestic—it's much more lower middle class, with much smaller homes. But I think Agrestic is really a state of mind. As Americans we've been mining the depths of suburban conformity since 1949, I would guess, a few years after the first one was built. I lived in New York City for eighteen years, but I'm brave enough to admit that I've drifted in and out of conformity. You can be living on Seventh Street between Avenues C and D in the East Village of Manhattan and be just as suburban-minded as anyone living in Agrestic. In many ways you can't get around it. You're conforming to a certain kind of aesthetic, or lifestyle—it's a coded, unspoken understanding of how to live there as much as anywhere else.

MARTIN DONOVAN has costarred with Mary-Louise Parker in *Saved!*, the romantic comedy *Pipe Dream*, and Jane Campion's *The Portrait of a Lady*, in which Donovan played Nicole Kidman's doomed cousin and admirer, a role that garnered him the National Society of Film Critics award for Best Supporting Actor. Donovan has appeared in such films as *The Sentinel* with Kiefer Sutherland and Michael Douglas, *The Quiet* with Edie Falco, *The United States of Leland* with Kevin Spacey and Don Cheadle, *Insomnia*, *The Opposite of Sex*, *Living Out Loud*, *In a Savage Land*, *Onegin*, *Heaven Hollow Road*, *Nadja*, and the Hal Hartley films *Amateur*, *Simple Men*, *Trust*, *Surviving Desire*, *Flirt*, and *The Book of Life*. His television credits include the FX movie *RFK*, USA's miniseries *Traffic*, and the Fox series *Pasadena*, as well as the television movies *Amy and Isabelle*, *The Great Gatsby*, and *When Trumpets Fade*. Donovan made his debut as a television series regular in the critically acclaimed drama *Wonderland*.

BEHIND THE SCENES:

Part One

WAITING TO INHALE:
THE PILOT

The pilot, written by Jenji Kohan, was shot in August 2004 and was given the green light by Showtime to go to series, which they began shooting seven months later. Jenji Kohan, Casting Directors Amy McIntyre Britt and Anya Colloff, Location Manager Paul Boydston, and Line Producer Mark Burley recount a hot and dry summer that yielded a bountiful season.

How did *Weeds* evolve from pitch to pilot?

JENJI: I pitched one line to Showtime in February or March 2004, and it got me in the door, and then I pretty much wrote the script in a weekend in April. We were shooting in August, so it all went pretty quickly. But once they said, "Go write the show," I went into a huge panic, because I was like, I know nothing about the subject. I have no idea what the show is. I have to do my homework. The first thing I did was read *Reefer Madness* by Eric Schlosser, which is a really good history of pot. Then I started asking everyone I knew about their experiences. I know a mom through my kids who had briefly been a dealer. I took her out for coffee and talked to her. I bent everyone's ear and let the pressure build, until I had to turn something in. Finally I just sat down and it was one of those things where I guess it was already there and I had to stop running in circles and let it come out.

Did Celia always figure into your idea for a show about a suburban widow drug dealer?

JENJI: Yes, she did. I wanted a foil, someone who was doing all the "right things" and getting nowhere to put up against someone doing all the "wrong things" whose life was working out to some extent. It's sort of like a chemistry experiment: You need your control group,

and Celia was my control. I was wary about a stereotype. I wanted a whole person in there. When we were shooting the pilot, someone mentioned that there was this other show in production called *Desperate Housewives*. I hadn't heard about it, and then I got really nervous. I think we're really different, and in the end it worked out for the both of us.

Who sits in on auditions?

ANYA: Amy and me, Jenji, Mark Burley, Roberto Benabib, the episode director, and usually the writer of the episode. Senior Vice President, Talent and Casting Beth Klein from Showtime signs off on bigger guest roles, even if it's two lines, like Allie Grant in the pilot, actors for roles we think or know will come back again.

Is a show about marijuana and grief hard to cast?

ANYA: Yes and no. With the pilot, casting rolled pretty smoothly, not least of all because the material is so good. People who don't normally audition for pilots were auditioning for this, like Kevin Nealon. It's all about finding people who can strike the balance between drama and comedy, because the tone of the show is very specific, and you don't want people who make something too big of it, because there are a lot of very sincere, sad moments.

JENJI: Kevin was originally cast as a one-shot. Originally he was sort of Nancy's agitator on the periphery. It's a good part, but I had not considered that he'd be such a full part of the show until we saw him in action and totally fell in love. Kevin just knocked our socks off. We had to make a deal with him and make him a regular character. This show is full of overnight sensations who have been around forever, myself included. I've been writing for television for fifteen years and all of a sudden it's like, "Oh, look who's here." A lot of people on this show have been around, but just needed to find the right thing. And we're always surprised at how many people we're reaching. I think part of it is that we all have low self-esteem [*laughs*].

No one was originally attached to the show. You landed two powerhouses in Mary-Louise Parker and Elizabeth Perkins.

AMY: Seriously. Mary-Louise was discussed very early on. The pilot's director, Brian Dannelly, had just directed her and Martin Donovan in the film *Saved!*, so there was a relationship there, and I think that's what really made her accessible, because she was not looking to do a series. She'd just done *Angels in America*, and had a continuing role in *The West Wing*. But being the lead in a series involves a long-term commitment. The material is so amazing, I think that's what ultimately sold her on it. Before Mary-Louise had signed on, Elizabeth was lobbying for Nancy. But once Mary-Louise was approached and her deal was closing, Elizabeth immediately switched gears and said very graciously, "I would love to do Celia if you would have me." At the end of the day she wound up with a role that is equally challenging, and equally spotlighted. They get to play off of each other. It's wonderful the way it worked out, because I really love Celia, and Elizabeth is fantastic in the role. I knew she'd be wonderful, but you never know how amazing it can be until it's executed.

JENJI: Elizabeth was so smart in her interview: We talked about Celia and she quoted back lines at me in character. You really got a sense of what she would be like as this character. She basically did the scene and it was very exciting. There was a discussion of whether she and Mary-Louise looked too much alike—I don't think so at all, but they made us dye Elizabeth's hair blond for the pilot.

Which were some of the harder roles to cast?

AMY: Heylia was pretty difficult because Jenji always said, "I know she's a hard-ass, but she needs to be warm," and we kept putting more of the hard-ass version in front of her without any den mother. The woman has to be tough, and run a tight ship, and I think it's part of her inherent nature to be a ball buster, but she's human and she's sympathetic when the time comes. We put some women in front of Jenji who we thought were really the right tone for Heylia, and she kept saying, "No, no, no, you're still not getting it." And finally Tonye [Patano] came across our path. She read on videotape from New York City before we had her out here to audition in person. She did the scene in the pilot where Nancy tells her she has to leave to take Shane to the grief counselor, and Heylia backs off. I saw that, and totally got it, because Tonye is inherently warm, but she can talk a good game. Truth be told, Tonye is too young for the role we were originally talking about, but she plays up the age as much as she can, and

through hair and wardrobe we try and put a few years on her. You don't have a crystal clear view of it until you put at least one actor for each role in front of the decision makers. Because you can talk about it ad nauseam—what's on the page, what you see—but it comes down to really hearing the words.

ANYA: Similarly, in the second season, Yael was probably the toughest to cast because Jenji likes the real deal—she wanted a real Israeli—and Meital is that person. She was in the Israeli army, and there are not a lot of actors out here who are like that.

AMY: And like Heylia, Yael's character was written as a little older. But when we read, Meital was amazing. She showed her commitment to getting this job by cutting a vacation short to come in for a callback. As casting directors, it makes us nervous that someone is jumping through so many hoops. It's one thing when you live in L.A. and drive ten minutes to come in for the fourth time, but she was jumping on a plane from Israel for a final callback. We finally gave her the job, and everyone was ecstatic. She's amazing—so sexy and so much fun, she really gets it. All of the sexual dynamics to Yael were met with open arms by Meital, which is great, because that is inherently the character. Someone needed to take Andy down a peg [*laughs*].

Who were some of your casting triumphs?

AMY: We lucked out with Allie Grant [who plays Isabel Hodes]. We had no prior experience with her and we didn't even have a full scene for her to read—we had two lines—so we cast her off of a vibe. But she was the right girl and she consistently delivers for them. Everyone had a gut feeling that she was going to work. Hunter Parrish has done an incredible job. He's really showing how much he's growing.

We are fans of actors, so for us, it's just fun to watch it all come to fruition. We are consistently pleasantly surprised by what they've done with the characters. They achieve our expectations and then go beyond. Now we can sit back and watch and have a good time. We generally love everybody. I really hate to single anyone out: Allie, Hunter, Alexander Gould, Romany Malco, Tonye, all of them. I go way back with Indigo. She's a spectacular woman in her work and as a person. And Justin Kirk's audition was like a eureka moment. We cast him so quickly, we almost feel like it was a fluke that he was in town and available and game for coming in almost all on the same day. It's so much

fun to watch, but it absolutely starts with the writing—Jenji came up with this incredible concept and really set the tone with the pilot, and everyone joined forces and works really well together, which makes our job a lot easier. The producers will not settle if they're not in love with somebody. The flipside is also true: If they see three people for a major guest starring role, and one person hits it out of the park and they all agree, they don't need to see other people.

The pilot was shot in southern California in August. What was that like?

PAUL: The shoot was a total of eleven days, which is standard for pilots, and we spent at least two, maybe three of those days filming in a park in Stevenson Ranch—the neighborhood where we ended up filming a lot of the show. That's where the soccer game scene is, and the scene where you see Celia and Nancy talking, while she's secretly dealing dime bags. August is a warm month everywhere, but we were in an unusually warm part of southern California—that area is sort of reclaimed from the desert in the first place. It was 105 degrees on the weather charts, but outdoors there was no wind, the heat was rising from the pavement, and the dirt was dried out and baked. It had to be 115 to 120 degrees in the sun, and there was no shade for the most part [*laughs*]. We were just dying—not a good way to start a shoot [*laughs*]. And the kids were having to run around in that. We had the special effects guys bring out these big fans with water sprayers on them, and we were spraying everybody down. We couldn't shoot anything in the shade [*laughs*]. It was a great group of people, and in many ways we had a great time shooting the pilot, but we're all bonded because all of us will always remember how miserable we were shooting those outdoor scenes in the park [*laughs*].

JENJI: My assistant at the time was trying to do this thing where he would try to walk ten thousand steps every day to lose weight. He decided to walk from the parking lot to the location, which isn't that far, but he almost passed out from the heat. There was no one on the street and it was really empty. He described it as wandering in the desert—he got lost because all the streets looked the same [*laughs*]. But our locations people were fantastic. We had Sno-Kone machines and big blowers and misters, and we put up tents. There was a carnival atmosphere because we were trying to do everything we could do to keep people cool.

Did you have to make any changes or sacrifices in the seven months between the time you produced the pilot and the second episode?

MARK: The pot had to be made greener in the pilot and indeed in the first season. For the dried-up fake pot, they used an herb of some kind. The plants are silk. In the first season we got some and they were not very good. If you look at the season one finale, that little plant that Conrad brings to the meeting looks terrible [*laughs*].

JENJI: We lost Quinn [played by Haley Hudson] and Josh Wilson [played by Justin Chatwin] before we got to series. I'd had this whole story line in mind for Silas and Quinn where we'd see their relationship in accelerated mode, going through adult phases in a concentrated amount of time the way teen relationships do and hit the midlife doldrums. Justin left because he was going to do the film *War of the Worlds* and be a big star [*laughs*], but everyone else was under contract. We hope to get him back for future episodes.

'scrips

The Writers' Room

Led by Executive Producer Jenji Kohan and Co–Executive Producer Roberto Benabib, the Weeds writing staff comprises eight entities and nine writers (two are a writing team, Coproducers Michael Platt and Barry Safchik). Six of the writers describe here the full writing cycle, from seedling to harvest: Jenji, Roberto, Story Editor Rolin Jones, Producer Matthew Salsberg, Supervising Producer Shawn Schepps, and Supervising Producer Devon Shepard.

Let's begin with the basics: How do you run a meeting and get the stories rolling?

JENJI: We all get together and break the whole season as a room to decide what's going to happen. Then we get more specific and cobble away at the details of each episode. Then we assign the individual episodes to different writers, who write up an outline. Once the outline is approved [by me and Roberto], the writers write their scripts. We get their version back and I will usually do a pass on it. Sometimes I'll bring it back to the room to see if there are any final thoughts, comments, or lines. I think my doing a pass on the scripts helps to maintain a consistency of voice. If I don't think the script is quite there yet, Roberto will do a quick pass on it before it gets to me. That's preproduction. Once we're in production, each of the writers follows their episode through. They come to casting; they are on set the whole time it shoots; and they're invited to editing. I like people to follow their work because people who are going to create good television have to know all aspects of how it's made, and I want every writer in my room to create shows. I love great writing and I love our writers. It is an island of misfits, but we're all supposed to be here for this and we found a home. It's a real family.

You've had the same writing staff for both seasons, plus Rinne Groff, who joined you for the second season. Have you worked with any of the writers before, Jenji?

JENJI: I've worked with Devon Shepard and Matthew "Salty" Salsberg. Everyone else, I read and fell in love with their scripts, and then I met them and felt they'd be a good fit for the show. Salty [who has written for *Entourage* and *Curb Your Enthusiasm*] and I worked on *The Stones* together and I absolutely rely on him. I worked with Devon on *The Fresh Prince of Bel-Air* years ago and we remained friends. I was introduced to Roberto by my agent—the best thing my agent has ever done for me. Roberto is, for all intents and purposes, my partner. He'd been out of the business for a few years (he most recently wrote for *Ally McBeal*) and was coming back in. He's been a godsend. I got lucky with everyone. Rolin Jones is a playwright from New York and had never done television. He's absolutely phenomenal. Everyone brings something different. Rolin always knows where the drama and the poetry is. Salty and [Michael] Platt always have the funny. Shawn (who wrote for *Rude Awakening* and *Encino Woman*) is always on the emotional tip. Devon can break an unbelievable story whole cloth. And Roberto keeps everyone on track. When we're having trouble with a script in a certain area, we can go to each person for a different aspect of the show. It's a really nice balance. I'm so grateful for all of these talented people who work to make this show great.

ROBERTO: I've never worked as well with anyone as I've worked with Jenji. What she finds funny, I find funny, and what she finds interesting I find interesting. Jenji is somebody I would be unbelievably close friends with even if we weren't working on *Weeds*. We really respect and love each other. And everyone in that room has a special superpower. Rolin is always talking about what story we're trying to tell, and that's absolutely invaluable. Devon will keep us on it, especially since we're all white and he's black. He'll say things like, "Black people don't think like that," [*laughs*] and it will stop the room dead, and he'll tell us exactly what we should be doing. But saying that would belittle his contributions. He's great at story, and very emotional. He came up with the whole mountain lion story line and broke it in the room. And every comedy writer I've ever spoken to has told me they consider Salty's coffee table joke to be the best joke ever written. You want a little of the voice of each of the writers. I can actually hear them. It's subtle, but it comes out through their modes of storytelling. A Salty script may stop the show for a great stoner conversation between Andy and Doug. A Rolin script might have this emotional through line. I tend to be story driven, so mine have a lot of narrative propulsion to them. Jenji likes to riff, so her characters may stop and talk to each other before moving on. You play with the volume. Everything is ultimately the same, but it's like an equalizer.

With so many people collaborating, it must get pretty intense in the room. What is a typical writing meeting like?

SHAWN: It's like a big Jewish dinner when we meet, where everyone is mad and screaming at each other [*laughs*]. It's like an eight-hour production of *12 Angry Men* every day without the malice.

ROBERTO: When Jenji got the writing staff together, it was like Noah's Ark: a giraffe, two hippopotami, three lions, and four tigers. None of us are alike. And working on those stories really requires the power of everyone together. You're sitting in a room with eight other people whose opinions you respect, and they're all weighing in so that when you finally go down a road, you're pretty sure of that road because anyone who could have weighed in with a contrary point of view has done so already.

ROLIN: And you can be a complete jackass in that room. There's no ridicule about ideas. There's ridicule about one another's personal lives—that's totally open. You can literally throw anything out there. You get to take risks. These guys all came from sitcoms and they are hilarious. I can't tell a joke to save my life, so it's really humbling to be in a room with all of them. It's the greatest day job you could ever ask for, and Jenji and Roberto have made me a better writer.

JENJI: We scream and yell constantly about different things. The best idea wins. It doesn't matter what level you are. At the end of the day, it's not a democracy because I have final say. But they hammer me. I had a ferret joke in one of the scenes and a bunch of the guys hated it—they think ferrets are cheesy [*laughs*]. Someone offered a pair of really expensive sunglasses to whoever could talk me out of it. After constant badgering I finally gave it up. You hired these people for their opinions and if everyone is screaming at you, you've got to consider it. You've got to be careful when people turn in drafts, though, because this is their baby, and you don't want to be too harsh. We've got to find a cohesive voice for the show, ultimately.

What kinds of things do you argue about?

JENJI: There was a huge debate about whether Nancy and Peter should get married, and whether Celia should arrest Silas. What rabbinical school was going to look like. Every plot point and every detail gets argued and run through in that room. You want to make your case passionately because you want everyone else to get on board, because ultimately they're going to have to write a draft of this. You need everyone to be invested in what they're writing.

Do you ever draw inspiration from your own lives?

ROBERTO: Yes. My wife died of cancer, and it not only impacted Celia's cancer story, but Nancy's loss of Judah as well. The show is all about truth, so everyone brings their stories in. Shane kicking Gretchen, that came from Salty's life. He said there was a girl he liked in grade school once, and he kicked her.

MATTHEW: The Yael story line is loosely based on a relationship I went through—*loosely*. The biter from season one was also taken from my life. To me, the funniest part of the show is when we use our own personal experiences. The little things turn into stories. I go for coffee every morning and I always see this guy on his Segway. I've never seen him without it. I named him Mr. Lippman after a friend of mine who is a big fan of the show.

ROLIN: When Peter yanks Silas's elbow off the dinner table, that was for my father. My father came from Long Island, and if you had your elbow on the table, he would simultaneously smash your elbow off and continue his conversation—it was very fluid. So when it came time to figure out how to turn Peter—because we knew we were going to kill him—I was very convinced that this would be the deal breaker for Nancy, hurting her kid like that.

Andy's masturbation lecture to Shane has become a classic television moment. Was the concept for that mapped out in the room?

ROBERTO: Yes, pretty much everything.

SHAWN: In the room we went through websites, looking up every possible word [for masturbation]. After hours of this, Jenji found a website so horrible that, as she read out the most disgusting stuff, people were leaving the room, one by one [*laughs*]. And that's a room of mostly guys! There was information on there that even our most professional masturbator hadn't heard of [*laughs*]. Jenji was yelling, "You're all leaving me? You can't handle this?" [*Laughs*] I'm sure Justin friggin' smiled when he first saw that script. Justin is not afraid of *anything*.

MATTHEW: Roberto wrote the monologue itself. It was pretty much entirely his. He gave a draft to me, and I think I added a line or two. But it was so brilliant when I read it. I was working on my own script—and when I read his script, with that monologue in there, it made me worry I was in the wrong business.

Writing a serialized half-hour dramedy is about as hard as it gets. What is the most challenging aspect of your job?

SHAWN: The page count is a big one—we have to be really careful about that because it's a half-hour show. The other thing is when story lines fall out at the last minute. You have to be very conscious that there is somebody ahead of you who is going to have to pick that up. It's all figured out in the room, but when it becomes alive and breathing, things change. Sometimes you have to bump a story up or hold a story back. You always have to keep an eye on the episode that comes before yours, to see how it might affect your own, and then keep the next person apprised of what's going on in your episode so that if something changes or moves around you can tell them.

MATTHEW: As a writer, I like to have my script be a complete work, so it can be tough because certain things can feel unfinished. It might take two or three episodes for an arc to be completed. On the other hand, it can make it a little easier because you don't beat

MATTHEW: My favorite joke was the coffee table joke. We pitched that in the room and it got a huge laugh. But my favorite moment in the series so far was actually a dramatic moment. It was in "The Punishment Light," after Judah's unveiling, and Andy and Doug are shooting up rats in the Botwin house. There was a comic montage, and in the middle of this absurdity Andy picks up a photograph of the boys and Nancy and Judah. And he just looks at Judah—there's no dialogue there. It's just a poignant moment of Andy missing his brother.

ROLIN: "Mile Deep and a Foot Wide." It's not a classic *Weeds* episode in terms of its comedy to drama ratio. In fact it's one of the darker episodes, but I love it. In the outline form, it was the "abortion" episode, which is typical of the assignments I get in the writing room [*laughs*]. One scene I'm really proud of is in "Mrs. Botwin's Neighborhood," and I didn't even write it, though I contributed to it. It's the "Be my friend" scene. I had written this really limp-dick, boring version of it, and it wasn't right. It was supposed to be the schism between Celia and Nancy, after which the two will no longer have any more drinks dates. Jenji rewrote it where Celia and Nancy kiss. Salty said, "That's retarded!" So we all sat around a table and tried to figure out what to do. It was a huge fucking war for an hour and a half. And then Jenji asked, "Can she pull Nancy's hair?" That was it! We all built it together as a team. That is the best part of the job, when it takes four or five people to put it together in the room.

DEVON: The scene where Andy and Doug are watching porn—*Incredi-hoes*—that's one of my favorites. A lot of my favorite scenes are written by other people. It's the first time I've been a fan of the show I'm working on. I think most of the writers on *Weeds* feel that way, and that comes through in the writing because you really enjoy giving your characters words. You're so involved with it. Even after we've seen it shot a million times, we still sit at home and watch it. That's a testament to the creativity of Jenji Kohan, bringing this kind of subject matter and these kinds of awkward characters to life.

rolling stoned

Directing *Weeds*

Veteran director and Weeds co-executive producer Craig Zisk—who works on such series as My Name Is Earl and Nip/Tuck—stepped into the role of house director in the second season. Zisk describes how to roll this particular kind of joint.

What does being the show's "house director" involve?

In addition to having directed seven out of twelve episodes in the second season, I also advocate for both the actors and the writers. During the first season, there were ten episodes with nine different directors, which was a lot of turnover. In the second season, I think that the cast felt like the consistency of my directing so many episodes helped them develop their characters a little more. From the writers' standpoint, I think I serve them by providing a consistent voice to help them make sure their words feel like the show, and by being someone Jenji can talk to, I can take her notes and ideas to stage, which I think made for a more cohesive season.

I also hire other directors, with the help of Mark Burley, Roberto Benabib, and Jenji. *Weeds* is a very difficult show to direct: With ten to fifteen episodes to do in a season, we can't afford to have a bad episode, so we are careful about who we bring in. I find in my work that directors tend to fall into three different categories: the actor's director, who is great with the cast but not as much of a shooter; the director who shoots something beautifully but isn't so great with actors; and the director who is efficient and knows what he or she needs and wants and can shoot quickly, which for

a show like ours is really important. But *Weeds* is rare in that we need someone with all of those qualities, and that's hard to find. We were able to bring back a couple of people from last season [Tucker Gates and Lev L. Spiro]. It's required reading for all of our directors to study the scripts of previous episodes and examine the directors' cuts to show them what we're doing. But we give our directors a lot of creative freedom. There's not one style to *Weeds*. We have certain guidelines, but in terms of being creative with the camera or finding a different way in and out of a scene, we're very open to it.

Does being a co–executive producer endow you with more responsibilities?

Yes. Just before the second season began, I started pre-production with the writers so that I could hear the stories and the character arcs, and help them shape shootable shows. It was really helpful. I'm also involved in editing and post-production. Jenji, Roberto, Mark, and I do everything from beginning to end. We shoot maybe thirty-two and thirty-four minutes of footage and cut four to six minutes every episode. The writer is on set and often in the editing room. Editing is really the third time the script is written, much like directing is writing, so it's nice to have the writer there to consult and make suggestions.

You often work on half-hour network sitcoms. How does a production schedule for a half-hour cable series differ?

With other shows I direct, like *Scrubs* or *My Name Is Earl*, we are doing twenty minutes of airable material in five days, but with *Weeds*, we have to create twenty-nine minutes of airable material in that same amount of time, so there's always this time crunch. We have four days to prepare, five days to shoot, and then the editor usually has some kind of cut three days after we finish shooting. Then the producers get a cut to take home and we start editing for about a week. After that we do music, sound, effects. From the prep to finishing an episode, it takes close to a month. We shoot everyday, so just as one episode ends, the next one is starting. At one time we might be in production or post-production on maybe three episodes, so one's being edited, one's being shot, and one's being prepped. It's a lot to do, but there are a lot of people to do the work. We have two phenomenal editors on the show: David Helfand, who worked on the first season and got an Emmy nomination for "Good Shit Lollipop." He understands the material, and is great with music [and] our other editor, Bill Turro, [who] joined us the second season and stepped right in. Bill is especially inventive. "Cooking with Jesus," which features the Mohasky Cup [marijuana convention], was the first episode he cut for us, and he came up with stuff that I wouldn't ever have thought of—he made it a lot better.

Weeds is a dramedy in the truest sense because it juxtaposes serious dramatic scenes with laugh-out-loud comedic ones. That must make your life as a director quite interesting.

I'm really lucky as a director to have writers who aren't afraid to put a larger-than-life comedic moment up against a heavily dramatic moment—most shows don't like to do that. They want to secure the audience a little more than we do. We find that it works, that you can have a scene where Andy is about to take a black dildo up his ass [*laughs*] and butt it up against a scene where Nancy's life is falling apart. That's one of the really nice things about the show: that we allow the audience to embrace it for what it is. It's a very delicate balance that I think our writers handle really well, and when it comes to stage, the actors and the directors really also have to find that balance so that it doesn't come off as being too ridiculous.

You've directed episodes in season two that have some of the most complex, chaotic scenes: the Mohasky Cup, the grow house kitchen scene with U-Turn [played by Page Kennedy] and the Armenians all pointing guns at Nancy. Those must have taken hours to shoot.

We work in a world of controlled chaos—that's just how we function [*laughs*]. I look forward to the challenge to do something big on our tight schedule and budget, and the writers couldn't be more helpful in making adjustments. An episode like the season two finale, where we have the grow house kitchen scene and Shane's graduation—well, it was incredibly chaotic. At that point I was directing my third episode in a row without any prepping and we were finishing up a season, so we had to finish on a certain day, and we worked a lot of hours. But the cast is always game to play. I talked them through everything so we were all on the same page and they knew to expect difficult scenes and that we were going to be there for a while. They know I like to work fast. I don't like to do a lot of takes or a lot of extra coverage.

The actors have to tackle some pretty intimidating scenes: Silas had a lot of uncomfortable encounters with Megan and Nancy; Celia verbally assaults everybody; and Andy is the master of the sexual overshare. How do you ease the actors into the material?

I like to talk to the actors a lot beforehand, especially Hunter and Alexander, because I can tell when something is going to be tough. Alexander and Hunter are always being pushed to

an extent that they probably didn't think they were getting themselves into and that's what makes the show rich and real. As we've said to everyone on the cast, "We're never going to ask you to do stuff that you don't feel comfortable doing." Hunter is very eager to learn. I always look forward to scenes with him because he's very thoughtful about the work and comes in with ideas, and though he lacks the confidence of a seasoned actress like Mary-Louise Parker, he approaches it with the same amount of enthusiasm to make it right. And he doesn't get buried in scenes with her.

It helps that I know the cast well enough to know if an actor is not going to want to do something difficult with another actor who might be a friend, but they all understand the importance of scenes and moments. That is one of the benefits of having somebody there full time: The cast is willing to go the extra mile because they trust me, and acting is about trust; if they can't trust the director, the writing, or another actor in the scene, you can see them pulling back a little. Making an actor comfortable, whether it's during nudity or physical dialogue, is my responsibility. The environment on our stage is very warm and receptive and giving from me down to the assistant directors and the director of photography.

Can actors weigh in with suggestions?

Yeah, I love other people's ideas. Sometimes they want to change things, and either the writers or I don't feel like it should be changed, and we discuss why. But the actors are reasonable and understand the show and want it to be great. I can't think of a time when either the actors or the writers felt compromised—the relationships on the show are so strong. We've used a lot of Kevin Nealon's suggestions because he's so smart and understands Doug, and brings a lot of energy and ideas to his scenes. In "Good Shit Lollipop," from the first season, when he's at the Bodhi Sativa Cannabis Club, he asks if they have any "Stephen Hawking" because he "wants to be rolled out of there." We probably did fifteen different versions of that line, but we used that one, which Kevin came up with. And during the Mohasky Cup, we made a spontaneous decision to have Kevin go up onstage—I can't remember if it was his idea or the writers'. But once Kevin got up onstage with the band, there was nothing that was directed by me [*laughs*]. He is one of the funniest people I've ever been around. He just took off with it and made it something. We were in the twelfth hour, and I was like, we have to use every frame of this—this is brilliant. Those moments are so fantastic. I think it makes the show more fun and the actors enjoy it. They really feel like they're getting to do things.

Allie Grant [who plays Isabel Hodes] has ad-libbed things that we've used. She always asks, "Is it okay if I . . . ? And I say, "Allie, whatever you want to say, I'm keeping a camera on you." [*Laughs*] There's an exercise boot camp, where Celia has passed out on

the lawn. All the women are saying, "I have stage-two diabetes," "I had chemotherapy." At the end of the scene, Isabel ad-libs "Okay, up-up, here we go! Everybody back!" Allie decided there needed to be a button on the scene and she just did it. I love her. We call her "Money" Grant because she always nails her scene.

Allie told me *Weeds* is the first acting job she's ever had. There might be a range of experience among cast members, but each is extraordinarily and uniquely talented.

They are one of the few casts I've worked with where we have a group of real actors. Their talent and skills are so strong, I don't find myself having to do a ton of takes just to get it right. They are always prepared when they show up onstage. Actors might not always be comfortable with their lines the first time through, but by take three, they're like, "Oh, I see where this is going." And then they see the episode and say, "Yeah, that *is* a great line," or, "You're right, that emotion *is* needed in that particular moment." There are times when I'll pitch something to Mary-Louise and she'll say, "That's not how I see it." We really work off of each other well. Mary-Louise likes to rehearse a lot, which I love. You get so much more accomplished in a rehearsal—you aren't discovering the scene as you're rolling cameras, so you don't have to do a lot of takes. That's not typical of

TV. I think the other actors really enjoy it because they can get their questions answered before cameras are rolling.

Elizabeth and Mary-Louise are the best I've ever seen act. I know how difficult it is at times for Elizabeth to have to say some of her lines because it's hard for me to have to read it. But then you see it on-screen and how it plays within the framework of the whole episode, and she's managed to embrace that. Not only did she get an Emmy nomination (and two Golden Globe nominations) but she is the character that's talked about a lot as a result. And Mary-Louise—those huge eyes—she says so much without saying anything that we often cut lines in post or as we are shooting. Sometimes she'll come to me and say, "I feel like I can act this line without saying it." And she scores. My favorite moment of the whole series is in "Cooking with Jesus," when Peter tells her, "I know you're a drug dealer." Her reaction in that moment is incredible: You see everything without her saying a word. She's scared, she tries to smile. It's all there and more. She really has the skill and we're fortunate that we have a lot of actors that can do that. We end up printing up almost all of the film [we shoot] because everybody is so good, and you can always find something that's special.

HOW nancy
DEALS

THE DOPE ON . . .

HEYLIA

ovingly dubbed the Rain Man of Weed by her family, Heylia James is legendary in West Adams for being able to "eyeball an ounce from outer space with her glasses cracked," and for making "everybody's business my business" ("You Can't Miss the Bear"). She has been running her family operation for twenty years, employing her daughter, Vaneeta, and her nephew Conrad Shepard, whom she took in after his drunken mother shot him in the leg. It was this tragedy, in fact, that inspired her to quit her job at Price Club and get into the field of green. The painkillers Conrad was prescribed were making him feel sleepy, so Heylia shook him from his daze with Purple Haze, got well acquainted with some of the higher-ups in the cannabis industry, and seized upon the lucrative opportunity to build a weedy little nest egg.

James

A consummate mother and Food Network devotee, Heylia nurtures her business much as she does her family—with devotion, protection, a great deal of tough-loving care . . . and some very savory dishes. Though she's very successful, Heylia is frugal and modest, only investing in top-of-the-line kitchen appliances and the necessary surveillance camera. She doesn't want to draw the world's attention, but she does have to keep tabs on the world. And with an eye on the future, Heylia sees in Vaneeta, her right-hand woman, focus, drive, intuition, and savvy to continue her legacy. Perhaps she would have had more faith in Conrad if he had a better track record: He and his white prankster friend Andy Botwin used to get caught up in a lot of trouble, stealing and getting summarily fired to-gether from Circuit City. Conrad can't quite grasp the fact that no matter how guilty Andy is, he will never do the same time for the same crime. For now Conrad remains Heylia's errand boy, whiling away his time shopping for car parts on eBay for his gas-guzzling hooptie. She recognizes Conrad's potential—he's shown her some very impressive hybrid

plants he's been experimenting with on his own. But she sees how easily he can be influenced by beautiful women, especially by her new client, Nancy Botwin, an Agrestic soccer mom by day, "baroness of bud" by night.

Nancy is just starting out and doesn't really know the hemp ropes, but she thinks she does. Her combi-nation of hubris and naïveté amuses Heylia, as do her stories, like the one about her friend Celia Hodes, whose million-dollar home is destroyed by a Coca-Cola–filled cargo plane that crashes through her bedroom wall. But Heylia isn't looking to be entertained by a client, even though she likes Nancy and sympathizes with a fellow single mother, especially a widow. Above all, Heylia requires loyalty and honesty from her clients, and as long

as Nancy abides by that, they're in business. When Nancy turns up short after Shane spends the night in the emergency room with a broken arm, Heylia says, "I'm sorry to hear that. Where's my money? . . . It's just business, baby. I know you got troubles, but like my mama always said, tough shit" ("Free Goat"). Heylia believes in collateral, not credit, and holds on to Nancy's leased Range Rover and engagement ring. And she'll just keep selling her the skankweed until she knows to ask for the call brands—it takes Nancy a trip to the Bodhi Sativa Cannabis Club to figure that out. As they build their relationship and Heylia feels confident that at least one of Nancy's feet is tethered to the ground, she begins to supply her with more than just weed: She offers advice on dealing and parenting her two boys. Sometimes they even talk about love. But Heylia James does not do anyone, least of all Nancy, any favors.

No matter how many precautions Heylia takes with Nancy, she can't stop Conrad from falling under the spell of her big brown puppy dog eyes. Heylia anticipates Conrad's hitting a slippery slope when he goes behind her back and gives Nancy Heylia's secret cornbread recipe so she can load it with dope. Heylia forgives him for that, infuriated though she is. But when Conrad beats up the security guard who jacked a $20,000

stash from Nancy and makes him return it to her, Heylia forbids the two to ever talk again. She warns Nancy, "From now on, if you got business to handle, you handle it with me, and if you got troubles you handle those yourself. You and Conrad havin' no more associations. . . . You brung out the stupid in him. Now, I don't think you told him to go down to that school of yours and beat the tar out of a security man, but you just blinked those big brown eyes of yours and there he was. And I can't have that" ("The Godmother").

Rather than scare them away from each other, Heylia all but seals their bond when she dismisses Conrad's proposal that they expand their business to farm hydroponically. "Heylia, I'm telling you, in order to grow, we gotta grow. . . . We can go hydro. We just need a warehouse. . . . I don't want to spend my whole life being a middleman," Conrad pleads, holding up his prized clone. She replies, "Please, negro, you still need to work your way up to the middle. . . . This is my business. And you work for me" ("The Godmother").

Heylia senses that Conrad is out looking for grow loans as he spends more time away from the house, but with Nancy still coming around she isn't too nervous about a collusion, especially since becoming consumed by her new interest in Joseph Mohammed (see "Heylia James's Special Bud: Joseph Mohammed"), a dapper neighbor who sells bean pies door-to-door for the Nation of Islam. Even though Vaneeta hates him on sight, Heylia sees in him a possibility not only for love, but for a new life of serenity. She tells Nancy, "I said, 'Call me,' and he said, 'I don't have your number,' so I says, 'I'm listed.' I haven't left the house in two days. How fuckin' pathetic is that? I just like him. . . . Even if I break my stallion, I ain't gettin' boo for Allah knows how long. Still, gives you a reason to get dressed in the morning" ("A.K.A. The Plant"). When the dinner party Heylia arranges for

Joseph and Vaneeta explodes in her face, however, she realizes that dealing is who she is, no matter how intensely she yearns for him.

Heylia gets back into the game at just the right time: Nancy delivers the troublesome news that she has a secret agent man—a DEA officer husband, to be sure—and he is planning to raid Heylia's house. Heylia recruits Joseph's help, and together they manage to foil the bust, though she and Vaneeta can't shake the feds, who are trailing them. They have no choice but to put the business on hold; Heylia takes a new job as a school crossing guard.

Infuriated with Nancy and terrified for her life, Heylia can't believe she's fallen so far out of the loop, but she discovers that it's even worse than she imagines when she hears murmurings of a hot new strain that everyone has except for her, and no one will reveal the source. She knows she can fish it out of her old protégé U-Turn (see "Nancy Botwin's Obstacle Courses: U-Turn"), the most fearsome gangsta thug in West Adams. Though he

dreads having to break the news, especially during his relaxing pedicure, he obliges her. "The strain's called MILF Weed. It's the brand of the day. Everybody love that shit. . . . Ah man, why I got to be the one to tell you the way it is? It's your boy Conrad. He and the white bitch got themselves a real game. They farmers now. And I got to say, they fuckin' great at it" ("MILF Money"). The betrayal is so profound, she storms over to the grow house and rips into Conrad. "There ain't no excuses for what you done here. We don't grow. We deal. That's what we do. . . . You went off with one of my customers and created a new game behind my back. You lied and you took business from me. That ain't how a grown man acts" ("MILF Weed"). With that, she he exiles him from the family. But when Nancy comes to her with an offer to sell the MILF Weed at a ridiculously low price, Heylia realizes that that DEA agent husband of hers is about to take them all down. "You two like those big companies pumpin' toxic shit in the air then actin' all surprised when the ice caps melt and hurricanes drown New Orleans," Heylia tells Nancy. "Fuck you, I drive a Prius," Nancy quips ("Yeah. Like Tomatoes"). Heylia decides there is only one thing she can do to make all of this go away, even if it goes against her principles. Make a deal with Northside Armenian Power boss, Aram Kesheshian (see "Nancy Botwin's Obstacle Courses: Aram Kesheshian"), to set up a hit against Peter Scottson. Save the family. And then pray for the best.

Heylia James's Special Bud

Joseph Mohammed,
played by Ron Canada

Love has found Heylia James in the form of a silver-haired devout follower of the Nation of Islam named Joseph Mohammed, whom Heylia meets when he comes door-to-door selling bean pies. Joseph brings out the girlishness in her as she waits around for his phone calls—when they do talk, her voice quickly shifts gears from brusk to coquettish. Heylia tries to keep the nature of her business from him as long as she can, but she knows it's only a matter of time before their clashing lifestyles and ideologies will emerge. As Heylia devotes more and more of her time looking on the Internet for couscous recipes and researching halal dietary laws, Vaneeta gets increasingly worried that her mother is too distracted to notice that the clients have been dropping away—even Nancy's visits have all but ceased. After Heylia has Joseph over for dinner, it becomes apparent that their relationship will never work when he criticizes Vaneeta for her braids, her tattoos, and even her single parenthood. Vaneeta takes this as her cue to dress him down, and stage an intervention with her mother.

Heylia finally comes clean with Joseph after Nancy tips her off about Peter Scottson's plan to bust her. She calls on Joseph to host a Nation of Islam meeting in her living room, and they successfully foil the DEA ambush. As the two part ways that afternoon, Joseph looks at Heylia in her traditional Islamic dress, and wistfully says, "The enemy of my enemy is my friend, Sister Heylia. . . . You sure look good in white." But making a life change for love is more than Heylia can handle. "So many rules," she says mournfully. "Ain't no way I could keep them all up for long" ("Bash").

RON CANADA has had recurring roles in The West Wing, Boston Legal, Jack & Bobby, and One on One, among many other television series. He's most recently guest starred in Brothers & Sisters, 7th Heaven, and Ugly Betty.

HASHING IT OUT WITH . . .
TONYE PATANO

What did you think of Heylia James when you first read the pilot script?

There are some roles that you study and there are some roles where you know the person. I know Heylia. I know who she is: as a sister, an aunt, a mother, a friend. I know she's ridiculous and goofy, I also know that she loves hard and *laughs* hard. But usually those kinds of people are the hardest hit. I was really crying in some of the takes of two scenes: the one where she confronts Conrad in the grow house, and the one when she says good-bye to Joseph Mohammed. Now, Heylia is not a crier. I was telling one of the writers about my grand-mother, who also wasn't a crier. The only time I ever heard her cry, it was the weirdest sound, and it was a heartbreaking thing. She was wailing. It was 1968, I was ten, and Martin Luther King had just been killed. The only other time I would see her cry was when she would listen to her spirituals, like Mahalia Jackson singing "Amazing Grace." I would hear that same sort of moaning, and in those moments, it was because she was happy. I see Heylia in that way. When something really moves her, it's not a cry of anger, it's that. Those are the kinds of people who have a tough exterior, and when you hurt, you hurt deep.

Early on, some critics had a problem with Jenji's portrayal of black characters. What were your feelings about it?

Jenji created this family based on her experience playing dominoes and so when you first meet a person or people you have an idea about, they appear larger than life. If someone wants to see my character or that character or my family as a stereotype, that's because that's where they are within themselves. The ironic thing is, the only people they are griping about being stereotyped is the black family. Every single person on the show—the Indian, the Asian, the Latino, the suburban housewife—they're all being typed too. The fact is, Heylia's family is just as valid and comfortable as anybody. I know many Heylias—not that exact human being, but she's bits and pieces of people that I know, and very specifi-cally, three women that I know very clearly, as well as parts of myself. Intelligence comes

in different grades and different forms. It's all intelligence. The language of the South, of uneducated people, there's a poetry, there's a rhythm, there's a way of communication that most people don't understand until you understand it. The kinds of things that the writers have Heylia doing are multilayered, whether it's watching the cooking shows, reading, making sushi rolls, or doing puzzles like Sudoku. Whenever you come to Heylia's house, you're always going to find something interesting and new, whether it's watching Heylia cook or Conrad go online to research hydroponics.

Heylia is a shrewd businesswoman and has imparted that wisdom to Vaneeta and Conrad. She appears to be much more interested in the business aspect of dealing than the product.

It's making a way out of no way. It's true capitalism. It's not like she's trying to sell a scam and getting her game going, and then buying every other thing. She's got her business set up, and she's been cultivating it for over twenty years. In my life, I know nothing about weed and had to try to bone up on everything, and on one flight out to L.A. from New York, I was sitting on a plane next to Tom Brokaw reading about hydroponics, and I'm

thinking, This is the epitome of the absurdity of life [*laughs*]. I was doing research, talking to friends who smoke pot, and I learned that a lot of people have the same dealers for twenty-five years. There's a relationship that develops. People who have been in the business as a dealer or supplier, it has a longevity, because it's not about the flash, it's not about any of that. To Heylia, what's most important is to keep her family together, and have a healthy home, period. The whole reason she's in the business is because she was taking care of her nephew Conrad after her sister shot him in the leg. She did it for her kids because family always came first. Right, wrong, or indifferent, that was the bottom line. She doesn't explain herself to anyone. Even if she's dead wrong, she never apologizes.

Do you think Heylia likes Nancy?

She does admire her and she's intrigued by her. Nancy brings weird stories from the suburbs to Heylia's kitchen. And Nancy always needs something or gets something out of coming to Heylia's house. At the very least she knows she'll be treated like family. There's a scene in the second season where she and Heylia were both talking about their love dilemmas, and it was an extremely poignant moment, and a different kind of scene than we've had before—I wish we had more of those. It does surprise me that Heylia has put up with Nancy as long as she has, because Nancy gets away with a lot of things. And what this woman can get away with and what we can get away with are night and day and we cannot lose sight of that ever. Conrad lost sight of that. The minute he started beating up on people, Heylia was like, "Are you kiddin' me? You don't do that unless you absolutely have to. If it's my business that's getting fucked up, it's one thing, but you're going to go out and defend this woman. . . ."

When Heylia learns that Conrad has started a grow business with Nancy, she feels betrayed by him and casts him out of the family. What did you think about her reaction to him?

I think Conrad has every right to want to grow, but it's that philosophy of, you may have taught me everything that you know, but you don't know everything that *I* know. And it was the way he set himself up. Basically he is putting her business at risk without telling her. I can respect a man who stands up and says, "You don't want a part of it—fine. I'm going to find my own partner." But he not only went behind her back, he poached her client. It's *how* he did it that hurt her. And on top of that, he put her in serious danger because

she didn't know about Nancy's DEA agent husband. That's a whole other thing. When he found out about that, he initially cut her off, but he went back.

You are considerably younger than Heylia. How old is she?

They've never been clear about Heylia's age, and I want the writers to get her closer to my age. I don't think she has to be an old woman. It's her essence of being and life experiences that make her older than Nancy—Mary-Louise and I are only a few years apart in real life. To me, it would be more poignant than trying to make me a fifty-five- or sixty-year-old woman. That's why I made the choice to take my glasses off in the second season. My mother had my sister at seventeen; seventeen years later she had me. My nephew was nine months younger than I am. Right now I'm old enough to have a daughter Vaneeta's age and a nephew Conrad's age.

Heylia is the one person who can humble Nancy. What is it like for you as an actress to do that to another actress?

It's a very interesting thing: My character, just by the nature of who she is, takes control of the room. For Mary-Louise to be that gracious and generous time and again as the lead in the series is difficult because every time she comes into that kitchen, she knows she is going to be made to feel stupid. That's very difficult for a human being, let alone a character and an actress. Mary-Louise is just phenomenal, period.

TONYE PATANO is known for her work in the Academy Award–nominated feature *The Hurricane* starring Golden Globe winner Denzel Washington. Her film credits include *Little Manhattan, The Great New Wonderful, Bringing Out the Dead, The Thing About My Folks, A Price Above Rubies, Fresh, A Good Day to Be George,* and *Messengers.* Patano's television credits include playing Laverne Owens in *The Jesse Owens Story, Highway Heartbreaker,* recurring roles on *Monk, Hope & Faith,* and *Sex and the City,* and guest starring roles on *Third Watch, Now and Again, The Human Factor, Deadline, New York Undercover, Law & Order,* and *Law & Order: SVU.* Patano appeared on Broadway in Neil Simon's *45 Seconds from Broadway* and in several Off Broadway productions, most recently *Ponies* with Michael Imperioli at Studio Dante. She has just completed a national tour of *Legends,* costarring with Joan Collins and Linda Evans.

THE DOPE ON . . . .

SHEPARD

Conrad Shepard has hit the "grass" ceiling in his aunt Heylia's business. No matter what he does—bring in lucrative clients, offer sage counsel—Heylia refuses to treat her thirty-six-year-old middleman nephew like anything more than her errand boy. If not for Conrad, however, Heylia would never have been inspired to quit her job at Price Club to start dealing twenty years earlier, when she was caring for Conrad during his recovery from a gunshot wound inflicted by his own mother—her sister. His painkillers made him too sleepy to function, so Heylia got him pot to smoke instead, which got her acquainted with the local entrepreneurs in the industry, setting her off in a whole new career direction.

To Conrad's mind, Heylia's business hasn't evolved with the times, and her adamant refusal to farm will doom them because Prop 215 has created a climate of proliferating cannabis clubs. Growing is the only way to survive. So it's little wonder Conrad diverts his energies to tricking out his hooptie, a machine that appreciates a little loving reinvention.

Then he meets Nancy Botwin, a recently widowed PTA mother of two, who gets him flying higher than he ever knew he could go. Referred by Conrad's old partner in crime Andy Botwin, Nancy is new to the business, an accidental dealer by way of selling dime bags of shwag to her dead husband's poker buddies. Without even trying, Andy's sister-in-law has cornered the entire market in the upper-middle-class suburb of Agrestic—and she's already in over her head. More than a few times, Nancy has come in short and been forced to leave collateral for Heylia. Conrad is struck by Nancy's odd mixture of daring, naïveté, intelligence, recklessness, mystery, and pathos—and she's stunning to boot. The strange combination of qualities may embolden her to expand her operation and open a cover business, but her lack of foresight and practical knowledge and her instinct to react instead of plan makes her a huge liability to the James family. Of all the occupational hazards they've navigated over the years, none has been more threatening to their safety and livelihood than this charming, careless, bourgeois soccer mom client from the private gated community. But Conrad believes he can enlighten her, and makes it his mission to endow her with skills that will match her grand ambitions. "Gives me a real sense of accomplishment workin' with overprivileged white women," he jokes with Nancy before focusing her on her next move. "You enterin' a whole new level here. Bigger buys, bigger risks" ("Good Shit Lollipop"). The closer the two become, however, the more he discovers the blissful ignorance in which she operates.

Despite this fact, Conrad interprets Heylia's wariness of his new friendship with Nancy

as a manifestation of their power struggle. But Heylia understands how easily swayed Conrad is, and can see the impression Nancy is casting on him—he's already committing small betrayals, like passing on her prized secret cornbread recipe to Nancy, who debases it by baking batches with cannabis butter. Heylia is determined to keep them apart after Conrad beats up a Valley State College security guard who stole $20,000 worth of bricks from her in a faux drug bust. "It wasn't your job to defend her," Heylia tells Conrad. "You fuckin' living stereotype of violence and stupidity. . . . You go up in there and beat the shit out of him with your little buddies for what? For her? So she think you're a big strong man. You're her fucking er-rand boy. And she don't know what the hell she's doing, growin' too big, too fast without knowing the lay of the land, and there you are standing under her with a big net in case she falls. But she gonna land right on your head, on my head,

and grind us all down in the ground. . . . You ain't seein' her no more. . . . You even see a white girl on television, you change the channel or I swear to the good Lord above, I will freeze you out so cold, you'll go to the North Pole to defrost" ("The Godmother").

Her message is received loud and clear, but it's immediately disregarded when Heylia dismisses Conrad's latest plea to grow, even as he presents her the beautiful clone of his newest hybrid. Nancy might be a menace magnet, but her belief and trust in Conrad makes weathering the repercussions of defection and deception worth the prospective business alliance. "Fuck Heylia," Conrad tells Nancy. "I've heard all she has to say" ("The Godmother"). Nancy lines up investors, money, and a staff, and instills in Conrad the confidence he needs to escape the stasis. Unfortunately, she has also started a romantic relationship with a single dad named Peter Scottson, who reveals himself to be a DEA agent. Conrad can't run away from her fast enough. "Don't you be comin' round Heylia's no more, you hear me?" he warns Nancy, who promises to end her ties to Peter. "You stepped in shit and you ain't gonna track it into my house. . . . It's too late" ("Corn Snake").

But neither of them can move forward without the other. Nancy, who has the money but not the green thumb, immediately kills the expensive plant she bought with Doug

Wilson and Andy at the Mohasky Cup, an exclusive, international marijuana convention. Conrad generates plenty of interest in his exquisite plant, but no one in West Adams will dare go behind Heylia's back to invest in his business except for U-Turn (see "Nancy Botwin's Obstacle Courses: U-Turn"), a radioactive landmine of a gangsta who appears far more dangerous than Nancy (he's been known to stab members of his posse for interrupting a conversation). Conrad is so taken in by Nancy and, even more, so eager to realize his dream that he goes against his instincts, and decides to trust her and accept her dubious assurance that she and Peter are finito. Conrad has wagered his family to put his trust in her; though she

intends to honor his high-stakes gamble, she finds that she is ill-equipped to follow through. Conrad tells her, "Baby, you never had any [moves]. Moves mean you think something through. You just been reacting" ("Mile Deep and a Foot Wide"). From the moment he rejoins Nancy's circus, he becomes infected with her bad luck and now the betrayals are just symptomatic of their chaotic, mad existence. Because every small triumph comes with an enormous price: Heylia exiles Conrad from the family after she learns from U-Turn that he got into business with Nancy. "You made a big mistake picking that girl over your family. . . . You lied and you took business from me. That's not how a grown man acts. . . . You a little piggy and someday a big bad wolf gonna huff and puff and blow your house down. Ain't no way I'm gonna be associated with you when he does" ("MILF Money").

As soon as Conrad and Nancy sign a lease to move their grow house into a residential cul-de-sac, they are welcomed with a farewell box of baklava from the neighborhood drug lord, Northside Armenian Power boss Aram Kesheshian (see "Nancy Botwin's Obstacle Courses: Aram Kesheshian"). The Armenian problem is swiftly taken care of during a DEA raid, which mysteriously leaves Nancy and Conrad's grow house unscathed. Conrad is suspicious of their good fortune and gets very uncomfortable when Nancy confesses that she's solidified a clandestine alliance with Peter by marrying him, which protects her but holds no promises to extend to her drug-dealing business partners, unless he decides to exercise goodwill. Nancy's attempts to broker a deal between Peter and Conrad only make matters worse because her new husband picks up on their palpable, albeit uncon-summated, romantic tension. The trouble almost seems worth it when rap legend Snoop Dogg christens their strain "MILF Weed"—naming it for Nancy—and immortalizes the love by laying down the tracks for a hip-hop homage to their hydroponic hybrid. MILF Weed becomes "the brand of the day," according to U-Turn. "Everybody love that shit" ("MILF Weed").

There is little time for revelry after Nancy tips off Heylia about a planned DEA bust; when the raid is foiled, Peter understands the breadth of his wife's deception and puts her on notice to turn everything legit. Conrad packs up his entire life into a duffel bag and readies himself to bolt at a moment's notice, but he can't quite bring himself to leave. He begs Nancy to make the marriage work for the sake of everyone's safety, but all hope is lost when Peter taps into their phone and eavesdrops on a particularly damning conversation. Enraged and seeking vengeance, Peter goes after Nancy, threatens Conrad, and demands that they sell their entire harvest to one seller and hand him the money. "What Viagra was to Pfizer," Conrad laments, "MILF Weed could have been for us" ("Yeah. Like Tomatoes").

Against Conrad's wishes, Nancy tries to make an offer to Heylia, who balks but ultimately decides, in the interest of saving everyone, to hold a secret meeting with Aram Kesheshian to arrange for the murder of Peter. Conrad negotiates a deal with U-Turn to buy the full MILF Weed harvest for the bargain basement rate of $300,000, but the gangsta has no intention of paying with anything but bullets to the heart. By the time everybody shows up in the grow house kitchen to claim what's theirs, the safe has been emptied by Nancy's older son, Silas, who has swapped out the weed with a cache of DRUG-FREE SCHOOL ZONE signs and dismantled surveil-lance cameras, leaving the two business partners to juggle the roiling tempers of a fully armed crowd comprising West Adams thugs on a thrill-kill ride, and Armenian gangsters, who are not leaving until they're compen-sated for the dead DEA agent parked in the garage.

HASHING IT OUT WITH . . .
ROMANY MALCO

What were your first impressions of Conrad when you read the pilot script?

Initially, when he was making the whole statement about Enron, I didn't find that part very profound. But when I saw how Nancy sought solace in him, and saw how he was there for her, I realized that this character was being fleshed out and I thought it was an incredible opportunity. He has this calming energy and he's the most sane person in the show. And given where he's coming from, he's a considerably evolved, insightful, warm, and genuine guy with a knack for something that doesn't happen to be embraced by the public, or I should say, the legal system [*laughs*]. I just thought to myself, This guy is probably going to be the first of his kind on television: a drug dealer who doesn't fall into any of the stereotypes whatsoever.

As a drug dealer he's not like anything we've seen before. He's a serious-minded, diplomatic, honest, entrepreneurial businessman who neither carries a gun nor indulges much in his product.

Exactly. Conrad is like what Jay-Z or a young Russell Simmons is to hip-hop; he's just not as flamboyant or vocal. He's the new age, the new game. He's where it's headed. Conrad's not selling in the neighborhood and buying fancy cars. He's actually approaching his business from a corporate perspective. He's well read and world-wise.

Conrad is clear-sighted for the most part, but he succumbs to Nancy's charms and it gets him mired in trouble.

A lot of the actions are influenced by the world that Nancy brings with her. I think a lot of the time he's trying to discern how much influence she has on his interests and the decisions that he makes. If Nancy was a guy, I don't think they'd be in business. But what she brings to Conrad—and what he is grateful for, whether anybody has written it into the script or not—is excitement, not just to drug dealing, but to life. At least that's how I try to play it. Heylia's house was a very controlled environment governed by her laws and rules. Suddenly he's

out from under her wing, and with Nancy it looks like the sky's the limit. She's selling him a dream, and he wants to believe it. But the sad part about believing that dream is the realizations and repercussions that go along with chasing it, because they're not ready to face them. I think this part of the journey is really a setup for much bigger accomplishments. Because even though Conrad's feeling Nancy, he's not afraid to use her as a stepping stone.

In the second season, Conrad is exiled by his family, his business partner marries a DEA agent, and he's punched in the face by Dean Hodes. He's not having an easy time of it. What was that like for you to play a man in such a state of crisis?

For a second, I actually took it personally and went to the writers and said, "Wait a minute!" I came to realize that Conrad was experiencing all that because he really and truly was a mama's boy. He had these huge ambitions but he'd always been under Heylia's wing, and you don't just come out of the gate and get it right the first time. He is going through exactly what he should be going through, and he is not really alone because Nancy is going through it too.

He and Nancy have gotten to a point where they're practically symbiotic.

Absolutely. With the arc that both of their characters have taken, whether it's spoken or not, there is no one else for them to seek solace in other than each other, because they've both alienated themselves from those who matter the most to them. Nancy's kids are getting less and less respectful, and she's slowly but surely being torn apart from every single person she's considered a friend or family member. Heylia made it pretty clear that Conrad is no longer in the clique. As a result of that, they are kind of forced to come to some form of agreement, and that's why they keep going almost there, then out.

Do you want to see Conrad and Nancy's love evolve into a fully realized relationship?

Now? No. I already know what's going to bring them together: success and money. It's going to make being together that much more possible, and that right there usually leads to the demise of a relationship [*laughs*]. I would love to see Conrad meet a nice chick who is somewhat intimidating to Nancy, someone ambitious who maybe even gives Conrad advice on other ways to make money. Just think, if Conrad hooked up with someone kind of savvy, who had really cool medical hookups and maybe even an overseas or Midwest connection, and she was giving him insight on how to legally invest the money to protect himself in the event that something went down—I'd love that!

In the second season you had some really combative scenes with Martin Donovan. Those must have been intense.

They were. Martin is a really good actor. He can make those words mean a lot—his cadences let the words sit there and then you begin to take things personally [*laughs*]. Those scenes between Elizabeth and Allie Grant are harsh too [*laughs*]. It's a great group of people. I feel really fortunate to be in a clique like that: Justin, Kevin—Kevin is just so special. Mary-Louise is like my sensei. I have been learning so much from her, trying to emulate her. All of this unspoken stuff I saw Mary-Louise do throughout the season—I made a conscious decision that I was going to do my best to meet her there. Elizabeth is so real and down [*laughs*]. I think everybody is still really grateful.

Who are some of your favorite characters?

U-Turn is definitely one of my all-time favorites, no matter what show. He is hilarious. Page Kennedy is a great actor—he really cracks me up, man. That "it's got the good fat" line—we did ten takes—I kept laughing in the middle of them [*laughs*]. I can't really single anyone out because everybody holds their own. I don't watch the show and feel like there's a lull when a certain character comes into play—anybody who ever opens their mouth on that show genuinely entertains the hell out of me.

Before you started acting, you were a rapper. What inspired your career change?

I was in music a long time ago—I had a deal with Virgin Records, and then I moved into music production. But to be really honest, after a while I felt like I had outgrown the types of people that I was working with when I was in that profession. I started realizing I had evolved into a different thing, and my passion for doing music wasn't there anymore. But

I've been able to extract some really good lessons from that business—it's perhaps the most ruthless business I've ever been involved in—because I used to rely on music for my happiness. It defined me. Now with film, I am so detached, it's almost hilarious. Rather than my life being a by-product of my career, today my career is a by-product of my life. I don't mean to sound corny. It's extremely liberating. Though I didn't have the most promising of careers, being a rapper definitely gave me a business edge and objectivity and a fresher perspective as an actor.

What's the most challenging part about playing Conrad?

I'm so used to being hired to be the funny guy, so it's hard playing the straightest guy. Sometimes I get this pull toward comedy, but I'm pulling it back. Keeping it subtle can sometimes be a little tough. It has gotten easier, but for some reason I struggled most in all the kitchen scenes. There's something really easy and natural about the way the dialogue is written and, as a result, I don't really have to do much. A lot of the times I don't get the joke until after the fact [*laughs*], like when I'm at home watching it on TV. I'm sitting there, laughing, going, "Oh-ho-ho-ho, shit!" I like that because I don't want to become self-conscious in the process of doing it.

ROMANY MALCO began his career at the age of seven when he picked up a microphone and started rapping, calling himself "Kid Nice." As a teen he formed the rap group R.M.G. and moved to Los Angeles, where Virgin Records signed them to a record deal after they changed their name to College Boyz. Their first big hit, "Victim of the Ghetto," went to number one on the rap charts. Malco made his transition to acting when he was working as a music producer on *The Pest*, starring John Leguizamo, who was impressed by Malco's gift of gab and encouraged him to pursue acting. His rapping background came in handy when he landed the lead in the VH1 movie *Too Legit: The MC Hammer Story*. Malco starred opposite Steve Carell, Paul Rudd, and Catherine Keener in *The 40 Year-Old Virgin* and is costarring in the forthcoming comedy *Blades of Glory* with Will Ferrell, Will Arnett, and Amy Poehler. His other feature film credits include *Churchill: The Hollywood Years*, *The Tuxedo*, *The Prime Gig*, and Jesse Peretz's comedy *The Château*.

THE DOPE on . . .

vanee

As the protégée and only daughter of Heylia James, Vaneeta has demonstrated herself to be an apt pupil in all matters marijuana, so it only stands to reason that she would be the heiress to the family business, even though her older cousin Conrad was the impetus for Heylia to start a dealing career when his mother shot him in the leg. But until new client Nancy Botwin—the suburban mother dealer from Agrestic—started coming around, Conrad was resigned to a slacker existence, hanging out in the kitchen with their cousin Keeyon (played by Tyrone M. Mitchell), bagging bud, and cruising eBay for rims for his hooptie. Not like Vaneeta, who has inherited her mother's business acumen, her pride, her tough exterior, and her pithy wit.

cial Bud: Joseph Mohammed"). He is not good for business. As Heylia surfs the Internet researching halal meats, Vaneeta is keeping her eyes wide open, and business is looking pretty grim. Though Heylia is too distracted to notice, Vaneeta suspects a collusion between Conrad and Nancy, which would explain why they aren't coming around as much.

Heylia wants Vaneeta to give Joseph a chance, but their dinner together proves disastrous. Joseph takes it upon himself to "educate" Vaneeta. "Your hostility hangs thick in the air. . . . Maybe you need to take a good hard look at yourself. Look at your tattoos. Your cornrows. Listen to the language that comes out of your mouth. You're not a lady. You don't act like a lady. And you wonder why your baby has no father" ("Crush Girl Love Panic"). Vaneeta hits the roof; luckily, Joseph has enough sense to clear out of their kitchen before things get really ugly. As Heylia admonishes her daughter for getting into it with Joseph, Vaneeta turns the tables, shakes her mother awake, and stakes her claim. "You so busy finding fuckin' couscous on the Internet that you ain't takin' care of your game," says Vaneeta. "Conrad's never here no more and business is off, and all you can think about is some fancy-preachin', pork-fearin' fat ass. Heylia, if you plannin' to drop out and become one of them lee-lee shriekin' Islam ladies, then let me know so I can hire a fuckin' babysitter and call Keeyon and get to work, 'cause everything's going to shit" ("Crush Girl Love Panic").

Heylia is heartbroken and angry, to be sure, but she recognizes that Vaneeta has come into her own and says what she needs to hear if there is any hope of their saving themselves before Nancy and Conrad inadvertently drag everybody down with them.

HASHING IT OUT WITH . . .
INDIGO

From the moment we first meet Vaneeta, she lets us know she's guarded, tough, and proud. But then we see her with the baby and she reveals her vulnerable, tender side. What do you make of Vaneeta?

I like Vaneeta. I think we have a lot in common. Like her, I'm not one to bite my tongue. I speak my mind. She's probably a little more blunt than I am [*laughs*]. She's abrasive, but that's a defense mechanism. Most people who walk around with that type of demeanor are usually pretty vulnerable when you get to the heart of it all. But I think she's a good person, and I enjoy playing her.

Do you think Vaneeta has what it takes to run the business if Heylia can't?

I think so. She's been watching her mother running that business for a while, which is why I think it was so easy for her to throw that out there as an alternative when she saw that Heylia wasn't on her game.

Vaneeta and Nancy have an interesting relationship that seems to teeter between caution and teasing affection. Do you think she likes Nancy?

Yeah, I think that the relationship that they have is a playful one. When Nancy offers Vaneeta advice on sterilizing and the baby, and Heylia is making a comment about it, Vaneeta says to Nancy, "Is that your baby? Stay out of it." I think that Vaneeta would bark at someone in her family as well [*laughs*]. Nancy comes over to their house and they mess with her, but it comes from a good place. Ironically, even though we are the drug distributors, we're probably the least dysfunctional family on the show. We sell weed, but we deal with one another, and it's evident that we care about one another and are very much involved with one another's lives. When Nancy comes to our house, she learns a lot from us.

Which scenes do you think best evoke the spirit of Vaneeta?

I like the scene from season one where Nancy leaves her keys, and I'm asking about her shoes, and Heylia tells her, "You better leave before Vaneeta strips you down." I felt like it was the first time you got to see what Vaneeta was like. I also like the scene where Vaneeta and Heylia's love interest, Joseph Mohammed, go at it. Prior to that moment, Vaneeta was like Heylia's sidekick. Heylia would say something, and Vaneeta would chime in with her two cents—they're comical together in the way they play off of each other. But that scene with Joseph Mohammed was such an important scene to see who Vaneeta really is. You see her personality there when she's facing him off in all of his righteousness.

Do you guys get punchy on the set being around so much fake weed?

Yeah, we're all crazy on that show [*laughs*]. Tonye, Romany, Mary-Louise, and I, we're like a family, so we're very comfortable being ourselves, and that's pretty much how it is on the set. We just act silly. We haven't done a table read since, I think, episode four of season one, but hearing the dialogue for the first time was just as shocking for us as it was for the fans [*laughs*]. The writers are crazy [*laughs*]. Sometimes I wonder if they're smoking weed [*laughs*].

You've appeared in recurring roles on *Buffy the Vampire Slayer* and *Boston Public*, among other television series. How does Vaneeta compare with the other characters you've played?

I used to get a lot of troubled teenager roles [*laughs*]. All of the characters were very strong—they spoke their mind—and Vaneeta is no exception to that. When I first read the pilot, I assumed that Vaneeta and I wouldn't have the same tonality or anything like that, so when I auditioned for the role, I made a conscious decision to change the way I speak, to change the tone of my voice—everything.

What would you like to see happen with Vaneeta?

Tonye and I used to joke around about how I'd like to see Vaneeta get out of the house. I was so happy when we had that one episode where she was out of the kitchen, when she and Heylia were sitting on a park bench with the baby. I also would like to have the opportunity to interact with the other series regulars on the show. I met Kevin and Elizabeth when we did the pilot, and I see them at the parties and premieres, but I'd love to work with them. I have to say, I feel like it's a blessing every day that I'm a part of this show. I think when we did the pilot we all knew it would be something special, and then after the response we got after the first season, we were like, "Okay, let's do this." People are enjoying it and we are too.

INDIGO was born Alyssa Ashley Nichols in 1984 in Los Angeles, where she still lives. At age five, she booked her first commercial for Armour hot dogs. At ten, she played opposite Louis Gossett Jr. in the Showtime film *Zooman*, adapted from the play *Zooman and the Sign*. She has had guest star appearances on such shows as *Sister, Sister*; *Chicago Hope*; *NYPD Blue*; *Crossing Jordan*; *Judging Amy*; *Girlfriends*; *Strong Medicine*; *Cold Case*; and *CSI: Crime Scene Investigation*. She has had recurring roles on *Minor Adjustments*, *Any Day Now*, *Boston Public*, and *Buffy the Vampire Slayer*.

Nancy Botwin's Contact Highs:
The Quick Fix

The Candyman,
played by Jane Lynch

The unannounced arrival of Andy at the Botwin house puts Nancy in a huge bind: Her clients love to "eat their smoke," "the gourmet fuckup" brother-in-law has made himself at home in her kitchen, and she is terrified that he'll catch a whiff of her business dealings and ruin her. Heylia gives her a quick-fix hookup, a dealer with a sophisticated, clandestine baked goods operation. The Candyman is nothing like Nancy could possibly imagine. She's a fit, middle-aged white woman with the humorless manner of a physical education teacher, who brags that she was once 314 pounds until she discovered exercise (and Weight Watchers, which she attends with Heylia—background information culled from the Weeds cutting room floor). Before she will sell to Nancy she makes the newbie dealer promise to exercise. "If you're a lazy fat-fat, I can't in good conscience sell to you," says The Candyman. "I'm hoping to put Heylia into a diabetic coma, so I have no problem selling to her. . . . Some people will never learn until their life is on the line" ("Fashion of the Christ").

Comic actress JANE LYNCH has guest starred in nearly one hundred television series and films, most recently in the Showtime series *The L Word*; the series *Lovespring International, Help Me Help You, Two and a Half Men,* and *Campus Ladies*; the Christopher Guest films *For Your Consideration, A Mighty Wind,* and *Best in Show*; as well as *Talladega Nights: The Ballad of Ricky Bobby* and *The 40 Year-Old Virgin.*

THE OFFICIAL WEEDS COOKBOOK

Agrestic Herbal Recipes*

WAKE AND BAKE: *Breakfast*

Hot Space Cakes

¼ cup of flour
2 tablespoons of baking powder
2 teaspoons of sugar
½ teaspoon of salt
a pinch of cinnamon
2 tablespoons of oil
½ cup of water
½ cup of milk
2 teaspoons of herb-infused butter

Preheat griddle or frying pan with a medium flame while making the pancake batter. Place all the dry ingredients into a large bowl and mix thoroughly.

Combine all the wet ingredients in a separate bowl. Mix well. Pour the wet mixture into the dry one and blend. Minimal stirring is required—the batter should be somewhat lumpy.

Oil griddle slightly. Pour batter. Flip the pancakes when the surface bubbles. Adjust the heat as necessary to keep the pancakes from burning, but the higher the heat, the lighter the pancakes.

*Recipes from the *Weeds* season one DVD. (For many more Agrestic herbal recipes, check out the *Weeds* season one DVD.)

HIGH noon: *Lunch*
Sativa Spinach Salad

1 bag of fresh spinach
1 can of fresh water chestnuts
4 boiled eggs, diced
1 onion, sliced
4 slices of cooked bacon, crumbled
2 teaspoons of the fresh herb of your choice

Add all ingredients together in a large bowl and toss with vinaigrette.

'SUP: *Dinner*
Ganja Lasagna

1 large package of no-bake lasagna noodles
3 cups of spaghetti sauce
1½ pounds of ground beef
1 pound of ricotta cheese
½ pound of mozzarella cheese, shredded
2–3 teaspoons of the fresh herb of your choice
2 tablespoons of oregano
1 tablespoon of sage (optional)
1 beaten egg

Preheat oven to 375 degrees. Brown ground beef in skillet and drain grease. Add spaghetti sauce. Mix the egg, ricotta cheese, and herbs together.

Arrange a layer of noodles in a lasagna pan. Cover with a layer of beef, then a layer of the ricotta mix, then a layer of sauce, and top with mozzarella. Repeat until finished.

Cover lasagna with aluminum foil and bake 15 to 20 minutes. Remove foil and bake an additional 15 minutes. Let stand for 5 to 10 minutes before serving.

BAKED GOODS: *Dessert*
Botwin Buddha Brownies

½ cup (1 stick) of butter or margarine

⅔ cup of granulated sugar

2 tablespoons of water

4 ounces of unsweetened chocolate

2 large eggs

1½ teaspoons of vanilla extract

1⅓ cups of all-purpose flour

¼ teaspoon of baking soda

¼ teaspoon of salt

½ cup of chopped walnuts or pralines (optional)

2 teaspoons of the herb of your choice

Preheat oven to 350 degrees. Grease 13 x 9 baking pan. Heat sugar, butter, herbs, and water in a medium saucepan just to boiling, stirring constantly. Remove from heat. Add chocolate; stir until melted.

Stir in eggs one at a time until incorporated. Stir in vanilla extract. Add flour, baking soda, and salt; stir well. Stir in nuts. Pour into prepared baking pan. Bake 15 to 20 minutes or until wooden pick inserted in center comes out slightly sticky. Remove to wire rack to cool completely.

THE munCHIES

Getting baked yields huge appetites, even for those who don't par-toke. Everyone has his or her own particular hankerings, but some people have more discriminating taste than others.

DOUG is the "chowhound" of the pack, boasting the most adventurous palate. A true gourmand, he detests chain restaurants, especially Olive Garden. He relishes Love Me Tandoor's bindi masala, sag aloo ("transcendent!"), and lamb bhuna ("I don't want to live in a world without this lamb bhuna!") so much that he orders twenty plates of it to go before the restaurant permanently closes its doors. Doug also loves Armenian basturma sandwiches and fatoush salads, and tacos from Tacos Guacos; and he waxes on about a plate of General Tso's chicken he once had in San Francisco's Chinatown.

CELIA loves food but tries to resist it, so her diet mostly comprises mimosas, martinis, Trim-Spa diet pills, and Ambien. Getting diagnosed with breast cancer, however, temporarily gives her carte blanche to indulge her ravenous appetite for fast food; she reveals a deep love of cheeseburgers, fried chicken, and ice cream.

ANDY is a master in the kitchen. Mr. "Fancy-cookin' Trouble" is a firm believer that "If you ever wanna get laid, you're gonna have to learn to cook at least one thing." Some of his specialties include eggs Florentine, osso bucco, grilled beef ribs, lamb chops, couscous, ratatouille, and paella.

A devotee of *Iron Chef*, **HEYLIA** is a culinary artist in her own right, and has invested her earnings in tricking out her kitchen with top-of-the-line appliances. With cravings as versatile as Doug's and skills as deft as Andy's, she is as likely to bake her renowned cornbread as she is to roll raw fish into elegant sushi rolls, grill gourmet cheese panini, or prepare a halal lamb and couscous dish to impress her Islamic object of desire.

ISABEL has a sweet tooth and loves to feast on peanut-butter-filled pretzels, chai lattes, and ice cream. But her true passion is chocolate . . . preferably without laxatives.

NANCY prefers liquids to solids, subsisting on red wine and caffeine in its various forms: hot coffee, iced coffee, lattes, and Diet Coke. She also likes the hot artichoke spinach dip at Olive Garden, Love Me Tandoor's bindi masala, Andy's paella, and Heylia's smoked-Gouda panini.

SILAS turns to grilled cheddarella sandwiches—no crusts—for comfort when anxiety runs high and his heart is aching.

SHANE guzzles fruit punch and Cactus Cooler sodas, especially when they're served up by Andy's ex-girlfriend-turned-kidnapper Kat. He also loves pizza eggs, Veggie Booty, and . . . bananas?

When she's not running on crazy, **KAT** sustains herself on cans of sockeye salmon and Red Bull energy drinks.

U-TURN might be a murderous thug, but he is extremely health conscious, feasting on avocados for "the good fat," and putting himself on the maple lemonade fast, which flushes him out and makes him urinate a lot.

THE BOTWIN FAMILY observes Judah's birthday by eating his favorite foods: chicken parmigiana and Almond Joy candy bars.

DOGG Daze afternoon
Snoop Dogg on the Set

Hip-hop legend Snoop Dogg made a cameo as himself in the second season episode "MILF Money," laying down a few tracks and christening Conrad's new strain, "MILF," named in honor of foxy Nancy Botwin. Snoop, with his full entourage in tow, put a potent spell on the cast and crew, giving everyone a case of mad giggles.

Can you get a contact high just from being in Snoop Dogg's presence?

MARY-LOUISE PARKER: Dude! [*Laughs*] I was like, "Whoa!" My son was there that day and heard about Snoop, and he wanted to know, "Where's the dog?" He really wanted to see the dog.

SHAWN SCHEPPS (producer): It was like Snoop and the carnies coming to town. The studio was a pretty small space. Snoop's posse included a white guy with a diamond grill who is his manager, another guy who rolls his joints for him, another guy who makes jokes, and the Bishop from *American Pimp*. I was sitting next to the Bishop, and he was wearing this whacked-out, stars-and-stripes clown outfit, holding a scepter and a gold cup, sloshing champagne all over the floor. He said, "Hello, I'm the Bishop." I said, "Do I refer to you as *the* Bishop, or just Bishop?" He said, "Why don't you come and check out my bishop?" I just laughed. He was like, "*Naaaaawww*, I'm serious. Why don't you come back to the trailers with me, and you and me can hang out a little bit." And I said, "You know what? I think I'm gonna stay here because it's my job." God knows who I'd be pimped out to [*laughs*]. It was like an opium den, the air was so thick with smoke. I know we write *Weeds*, but we're not weed smokers. We were all getting contact highs. It all felt so crazy till Snoop got up to the mic. That guy is so charismatic, and has mad skills. The second he started rapping, everybody just froze because he became a completely different person. He was ripping out the "MILF" song, pulling the shit out of the air.

CRAIG ZISK (director): Snoop really wanted to rehearse; he was really concerned about the acting. It was not what I expected. I kind of thought he'd be one of those guys who would say, "Tell me where to go. Do I stand here?" But he really wanted to work the scene out with Mary-Louise and Romany and the other actors. I was very impressed by that, and really respected that he wanted it to be good. When we got to the actual rapping, we were all, well, rapt.

Jenji wrote the rap. Did he riff off of that? Or did he come up with a couple of his own versions?

CRAIG: Jenji had written great lyrics for the actual rap that he'd done in the studio, and then he asked, "Do you mind if I enhance words and change them up a little?" Jenji was like, "No problem." So he did her version, and we did one take of that, and it was great. Then he asked, "Can I go again?" And basically he made up the rap, and it was brilliant. I asked him if he wanted to do another, and he came up with a completely different one. He ended up doing three versions and they were all very intense. You could really see the artistry of rap. I was so impressed by it and he was so nonchalant about it. He just nailed it, and we shot all three in an hour. It was a great day. He was such a champ and his guys totally added to the scene. I wish I'd had more shooting time and screen time to really delve a little deeper into their world, but what we got was amazing, and it became one of my favorite scenes to do this past season.

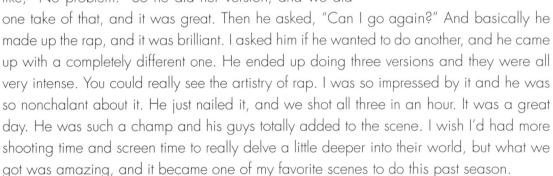

MARY-LOUISE: We had so much fun. After he did the improv rap, he did this rap for me, and it was probably the biggest compliment that was ever paid to me in my life [*laughs*]. My friend was there, and he was standing next to him, and [Snoop] said, "I'd do her." And I was like, "Why didn't anyone tell me that? I need to hear these things. I'm forty-two years old!" [*Laughs*] On IMDb it says I have a song written for me by Counting Crows, but now I have a rap! I have to say, Snoop is a lovely fella—I really liked him.

THE DOPE ON . . .

Nancy Botwin's Contact Highs:
The Accountant

DOUG

WILSON

Judah may not have left Nancy any money, but he did leave behind a good friend and financial manager in Doug Wilson. A self-described "idiot savant" ("Free Goat") when it comes to accounting, Judah's old poker buddy does everything he can to keep Nancy's coffers full. One of her most loyal customers, "City Councilman Doug" has hooked her up with all of his stoner pals, helping her to become the biggest game in Agrestic. Doug, together with his best friend, lawyer Dean Hodes, finds her retail space for her sham bakery through which she can launder money so she can pay her bills, and a house for the grow business she starts with Conrad, eventually becoming one of Nancy's business partners—few things give Doug more pleasure than knowing he is getting paid for weed!

Through Nancy, Doug meets a pothead kindred spirit in her slacker brother-in-law, Andy, who has crash-landed in her home. The two first connect while smoking and watching *Incredi-hoes*—their porn of choice—and debating over the "thing between the dick and the asshole" (Doug says "runway"; Andy says "taint," because "'tain't ass, 'tain't equipment"; Lupita shuts them both down with her answer: "the coffee table") ("'Lude Awakening"). When they spend the night after Judah's unveiling smoking and shooting at a rat running through the wall of the Botwin house, they have consummated their surrogate brotherhood.

Beloved in Agrestic for his oafish, easygoing manner, Doug is actually more complex than he lets on. He wants his position on the Agrestic City Council to define him, but he revels in his political apathy, voting Republican simply because First Lady Laura Bush sold him some good shit back in college. And even though he can't remember whether the United States invaded Iraq or Iran, he is an impassioned, incredibly opinionated gourmand, with a sophisticated palette and a particular appreciation and distinctive knowledge of the cuisines of Asia and the Middle East.

But Doug's dopey facade belies the depth of his pain—smoking is like his emotional morphine drip. His wife, Dana, is a stripper/fitness instructor who prefers rubbing herself against the go-go pole installed in their bedroom to riding him. And he has no relationship with his teenage son, Josh (see "Doug Wilson's Kif and Kin: Josh Wilson"); if he did, he'd discover Josh is not only gay, but selling pot to Agrestic's under-twenty-one crowd. While Doug wouldn't exactly be thrilled

about Josh's sexuality, he'd be infuriated to learn that his own son has been holding out on him.

But city council is one realm in which Doug feels like suburban royalty. He can "park anywhere," get "cutsies in every line—the bank, the movie theater, Hop Fung's"—and score "the three-item combo for the price of two. I [also get] to drive the fire truck" ("Must Find Toes"). Among the most gratifying perks of his position: He can use his power to taunt Celia Hodes, his mortal enemy. He opens Pandora's box, however, when he denies her many requests for a traffic light after she survives a car crash at the busy intersection, instead allocating funds to renovate the city council chambers, host a parade, and pay a branding firm for the new town slogan: "Agrestic: the Best of the Best-ic." Celia decides to challenge Doug in the upcoming city council election, which enrages him. "I run unopposed," he tells Celia. "This is my thing! Get your own thing" ("Corn Snake").

Angry though he is, he feels confident of the support he has from the citizens of Agrestic, and is certain he can win the election. After all, Celia's own husband is on Doug's side, opting to work as his campaign manager. Doug's campaign slogan, "Change Just Brings Problems," ("A.K.A. The Plant") resonates with Agrestic voters, who are Doug loyalists, as Celia discovers when she campaigns door-to-door. Doug doesn't even prepare for their upcoming debate because, as he tells Dean, "I could stand up at that podium and take a shit on one of those Make-A-Wish cancer kids, and the people would still vote for me. 'Cause they hate your wife. And I'm likable" ("Mrs. Botwin's Neighborhood").

161

In a bitter twist of fate, Dean forgets to file Doug's intent-to-run papers; Celia's is the only name that appears on the ballot. Being relegated to write-in candidate status costs him the election, so what choice does he have but to dump Dean for "ruining [his] life" ("Must Find Toes")? City council is the "only thing in [his] life [he] didn't have to get baked to get through" ("Bash"). It gave Doug a sense of purpose, and without it he is feeling unmoored, and bored enough to turn up at the city council meetings with the intent of heckling Celia, who is antagonizing the community with her antidrug crusade as she installs surveillance cameras throughout the town.

Doug surprises himself when he starts giving Celia advice about how to navigate the interpersonal politics of Agrestic. Nothing could be more shocking, however, than the incendiary affair that develops between them after an informational meeting leads to a spontaneous screwfest on his office desk. The two archenemies start meeting for daily assignations at the local no-tell motel, having wild, passionate sex and watching the fascinating footage of Agrestic's citizens' late-night activities. Soon the thin line between love and hate has been dissolved, and Celia announces she will leave Dean if he will leave Dana. She upholds her end of the bargain, but Doug can't quite bring himself to end his sexless marriage. He tells Celia, "You know, Dean used to talk about the terrible things you'd say to him. The horrible way you'd treat him. Dana won't fuck me, but she's a sweetheart. It's nice to live with sweet. You're not sweet" ("Yeah. Like Tomatoes").

His damaged friendship with Dean now irreparable, and his relationship with Celia returned to its state of enmity, Doug's unexpected affair demonstrates that change really does bring problems.

Doug Wilson's Kif and Kin

Josh Wilson,
played by Justin Chatwin

Doug Wilson doesn't know it, but his smart-alecky teenage son, Josh, is the premier pot dealer to all of the high school kids in Agrestic. When Josh's supplier leaves for vacation without filling his orders, he calls Nancy to hook him up. She begrudgingly obliges him as long as he promises not to sell to middle school kids. He promises her "if they're too young to bleed, they're too young for weed. No grass in the field? No grass will they yield" ("You Can't Miss the Bear"). When Nancy learns that a ten-year-old gets busted for carrying pot in his lunch box, she goes after Josh. But he calls Nancy on her hypocrisy, and she realizes there is nothing she can do to stop him . . . that is, until she discovers that Josh is having an affair with her much older neighbor, Hiram. Threatening to out Josh to his dad is exactly what she needs to keep Josh in check.

JUSTIN CHATWIN costarred in the film *War of the Worlds* and has guest starred in the television series *Lost*, *Smallville*, *Just Cause*, and the miniseries *Christy: Choices of the Heart*.

What were your first impressions of Doug when you read the pilot script? Was your mind spinning with ideas of what to do with him?

Yes. I thought he was a perfect character for me to play. I read a few pilots that season and nothing really struck me as being that good. And then when I read Doug Wilson, I thought, "Boy, I can play this guy." [*Laughs*] I saw all of his foibles and that little boy in him. It was one of those things where I knew exactly what I wanted to do with it and it came pretty easily to me too.

How would you describe him?

Doug is a big kid. He doesn't seem to have a valve on him that regulates propriety. He smokes more pot than he should. He has trouble with his willpower, not that he even wants to activate his willpower. He's a good accountant, and he's typically liked by a lot of people. Doug's an easygoing guy who doesn't take a lot of things seriously. And he likes to have a good time. But pot is very important to him.

You make Doug so easy to love, and in part I think it's because you gingerly expose him as a heartbroken, lonely guy. There's a reason he's baked all the time.

He is kind of a sad character in a way, always trying to choose between right and wrong, and usually choosing to do what he wants to do instead of doing the right thing. Some of his pain definitely comes from his marriage, which isn't a very happy marriage—his wife is a pole dancer who is not satisfying him sexually. And he's got a wild son, who we only saw in the pilot [*laughs*]. I think he's probably numbing all his discontent with marijuana.

And similarly, he is totally invested in being "City Councilman Doug," which gives him a sense of importance.

Yeah, and I don't think Doug realized it was an option for him to lose that election, or how much that position meant to him. It really is his ace in the pocket. That got him the nice table in the restaurant, and the ability to ride on the fire truck. That was a big upset for him.

Have you ever met anyone like him in life?

I've never met a professional like Doug who smoked that much weed. I've had roommates who were potheads, but they weren't accountants, or didn't handle other people's money in businesses in that respect. But it's amazing how many people smoke pot who do have responsible jobs. I think a lot of us, like Doug, are always trying to decide between doing what we want to do and doing the right thing.

What's the most challenging aspect of playing Doug?

That honey rose herb we have to smoke—it is hard on the throat, physically. Even though it's not pot, if you don't smoke, any time you inhale smoke it makes you light-headed. In that scene when Justin [Kirk] and I were smoking on the couch, watching *Incredi-hoes* and doing a lot of takes, I couldn't get off the couch after smoking the stuff. I had a big smile on my face, I was so light-headed. We had to ask them what was in the stuff. Pot would have been less harsh on our lungs. Real porn, fake pot. Aside from the fake pot, though, any scene that's emotional is pretty challenging. When I lost the election, and Dean came in and told me he screwed up and I had to get really angry at him, I had to go to places inside my head that brought up different emotional things, which I think is hard for any actor to do. I'm usually playing a comedic role, so it's easy to get to it but not always pleasant to be there.

You are responsible for some of the most hilarious scenes in the series. You look like you're having a blast.

I loved being on the megaphone and telling everyone that Celia Hodes had chlamydia. The Mohasky Cup was really fun too, dancing on the stage with the reggae band. We've gotten into some laughing fits where we couldn't even look at one another, and it had nothing to do with the honey rose herb. When you're around sets for a long time and you're tired, and you kind of step back and you see the silliness of it all, something triggers it.

Do you get to improvise?

Sometimes. When we were in that medical marijuana Bodhi Sativa place, I ad-libbed and came up with a bunch of different names for strains. I think we settled on the "Stephen Hawking" because "I wanted to be rolled out of there." And then there was that scene where I was sniffing the Magic Marker. I did a whole bunch of takes on that. [Sniffing] "Ah, Boy Scouts." [Sniffing] "Den leader." "Pack leader." Then I said: [Sniffing] "Lifeguard, Bridgeport, Connecticut." I had been a lifeguard in Bridgeport, and they used that one. There isn't too much room for ad-libbing, but the writers are so cool; they'll come up to you and say, "Got any ideas for this?" They'll get the shot that they've written, and then do some extra takes just to have them.

You launched your career doing skit comedy on *Saturday Night Live*, so it must be an interesting experience to work on a series, playing a character who is developed over time.

Yeah, there's something really nice about it. I do take the other route so much—character act-ing, stand-up, skit comedy—that playing something so established is fun and I can also bring my own little nuances and history to it. And I'm not cornered into this one character on a TV show: I write at home. I do stand-up. I do movies here and there. I did an episode of *Fat Actress* and *Curb Your Enthusiasm*, which were both kind of improv and that was a lot of fun.

Things get really physical for you in season two: You have hot-and-heavy sex with Celia and engage in a drool battle with Dean.

Elizabeth was always coming up with great ideas. That love scene we did—if you want to call it a love scene, with the barking—we didn't want to just make it another sex scene; we wanted to have sex in a funny way. She's such a great actress, makes great choices. And spitting drool on Dean was great. Everybody was feeling so crappy about every situation they were in at that graduation. It's an interesting group of people and relationships. The second season really made a nice turn where they explored those relationships a lot more. I mean, who would have thought Doug would have ever come in contact with Celia or Conrad? But nothing really surprises me on that show. I'm ready for anything. I think if I ended up killing somebody in the third season, it wouldn't surprise me, because the characters go in all different types of directions.

It must have been unsettling to have to drop the C-bomb in front of little Isabel Hodes.

It *was* difficult for me. Some of the dialogue the kids have to say is so obscene. In fact, when we used to have table reads during the first season, there were points where the kids had to leave the room. And there were scenes where *I* would have liked to have left [*laughs*]. My parents don't watch the show at all. I tell them if they watch it, they'll never see me in the same light again.

What's it like being on the set?

It's fun hanging out with everybody in between takes. I enjoy being with Mary-Louise and her three-year-old son, Will. She brings him to the set, and he's the cutest little kid. Everybody is just so interesting and fun to be with. I've had dinner with almost everybody on the set in the off hours. Jenji Kohan is just a blast. Andy Milder lives only a mile away from me. Romany Malco lives not too far away from me too, down near the South Bay, and I think everybody else lives up in the L.A. area except Mary-Louise and Tonye Patano.

Do you have a favorite character?

I really love a lot of the characters on the show, but I think one of my favorites is Renée Victor's character, Lupita. She's hilarious, and she's really taken advantage of holding that information out. She's got a great reaction in the coffee table scene.

Have you been mistaken for a stoner?

Definitely. I do a lot of stand-up around the country, and invariably somebody comes up to me after a show and asks me if I want to go out and smoke pot. They just assume I'm a pot smoker, and I'm not. I mean, I've smoked pot before, but I didn't exhale, so it might still be in there. The demographics the show reaches is amazing. I'll have a twenty-year-old come up to me and say, "Dude, I love *Weeds!*" and then I'll have a seventy-five-year-old woman at the mall say, "I love your show!" and a thirty-five-year-old professional guy saying, "Lovin' it. Lovin' it." People ask me all the time what's going to happen from week to week.

I'm assuming you're nothing like Doug, right?

[*Laughs*] I think I'm much more thoughtful and more compassionate than Doug. I will go out of my way for people. I'm a registered Independent, and I've never bought weed from Laura Bush [*laughs*]. I couldn't believe that line got through legal. . . . That just goes to show you that America *is* what it's cut out to be.

KEVIN NEALON, a cast member of *Saturday Night Live* from 1986 to 1995, is most recognized for the characters he created, including the Subliminal Man and Hans and Franz, and for anchoring "Weekend Update." Nealon's extensive television credits include guest appearances on such award-winning shows as *The Larry Sanders Show*, *Fat Actress*, *Curb Your Enthusiasm*, *Third Rock from the Sun*, and Comedy Central's *Crank Yankers*. Nealon, who made his film debut in the 1987 romantic comedy *Roxanne* with Steve Martin, has gone on to star in more than two dozen comedies, including *Happy Gilmore* and *The Wedding Singer*, both with Adam Sandler; *Joe Dirt*; and *The Master of Disguise*. More recently Nealon was seen in *Anger Management* with Jack Nicholson, *Daddy Day Care* with Eddie Murphy, and *Good Boy* with Molly Shannon. Nealon also stays busy performing stand-up comedy around the country and can be seen in his own stand-up special on Comedy Central. In addition to his acting credits, Nealon is an established and acclaimed writer, which has garnered him an Emmy nomination for his work on *Saturday Night Live*.

THE DOPE ON ...

Sanjay

Valley State College commuter student Sanjay is a self-described "highly intelligent underachiever with debt" ("Higher Education") paying his way through school, living at home with his Indian family, and resigned to a life of appeasing his parents. But then he meets Nancy Botwin, and everything veers off course—much to his delight. Originally hired to tutor her older son, Silas, Sanjay is offered an opportunity to take a detour when Nancy asks him to sell pot on campus. Though the virginal Sanjay is terrified of entering the illicit realm of dealing drugs, his burgeoning crush on Nancy emboldens him to push on and thrive as her foot soldier. He even recruits three of his siblings to join the sales force.

Soon Sanjay is sampling the greenery, which Nancy discovers when he shows up uncharacteristically late for their stash exchange and tries to kiss her. Spying an on-campus security guard charging toward them, he also reveals his mettle deficiency when he flees, leaving Nancy holding the bag and getting

busted. Desperate to make amends, a sheepish Sanjay turns up at the new "fakery," Breadsticks & Scones, and presents Nancy with, of all things, a gift basket full of cookies. "How can I make it up to you?" he pleads. "I'll do anything. Please. I might be a coward, but I love you" ("The Punishment Lighter"). She saddles him with all of the fakery tasks that flaky Andy was supposed to do: baking the goods, waiting on customers, working the cash register, managing inventory. He voluntarily adds to his responsibilities guarding Nancy's virtue by subjecting her love interest, Peter Scottson, to a merciless inquisition as he tries to order a muffin: "What are your intentions with Nancy? . . . She's a remarkable woman. Strong yet feminine. Brave and bold with beautiful skin. . . . Do you love her?" ("The Godmother").

As Sanjay bitterly hauls heavy groceries from Nancy's Range Rover into the fakery kitchen one afternoon, he overhears Conrad propose to Nancy that they liquidate Breadsticks & Scones and bail out of the lease, which would give them half of the seed money for the grow house. Sanjay is almost as intrigued by the conversation as he is jealous of Conrad for being able to call Nancy "baby," and demands to know why he assumes the privilege. "It's a black thing," Conrad explains. "I'm . . . not white," Sanjay says. "You ain't black, neither" ("Corn Snake"). Eager to win Nancy's heart and Conrad's respect, Sanjay burns down Breadsticks & Scones, making it look like an accident; the insurance money they collect gives them everything they need to start the grow house. Not even the fire can garner Sanjay the attention of Nancy, though he does earn her cautious gratitude: She rewards him with a generous bonus; but he still can't call her "baby." But he remains devoted to the cause, if only because he enjoys being part of a clique. Yes, he has to endure a bit of hazing—annoying ethnic jokes from Conrad and Andy, and grueling all-night watchman shifts at the grow house—but Sanjay rolls with it. To him it's a small price to pay for the chance to hang with the big guys and gain proximity to the object of his affection.

Sanjay even appears to be shedding a thin layer of cowardice after his near arrest during the DEA raid of the grow house neighborhood, as he and Andy frantically if stupidly attempt to flush all of the plants down the toilet before scurrying into closets to hide. When he suffers through the gruesome experience of sticking his fingers up a ferocious pit bull's anus in a failed effort to save Andy's toes, he and the guys are practically bonded for life. Sanjay treasures his secret home away from home, where he can do some soul-searching, make an ass of himself in good company, and learn the kind of life lessons they don't offer at Valley State College, let alone in his parents' house. And from this humiliation comes evidence that lots of things can sprout in the grow house, perhaps even cojones.

Sanjay may have a chance to put them to the test when Conrad and Nancy hold a meeting to sell off their last harvest of MILF Weed to U-Turn (see "Nancy Botwin's Obstacle Courses: U-Turn"), and banish him to the grow house closet to hide. They instruct Sanjay not to come out under any circumstances. But the sale quickly turns into a disaster—the Armenians have been hired to kill Peter and await payment from the money Conrad would have gotten from U-Turn, who has decided instead to jack the farmer and the MILF, except that the weed is MIA. With all guns pointed at Nancy, will Sanjay heed their warning to stay in the closet, or will he emerge the hero and save the day?

Hashing it out with...
maulik pancholy

What do you think of Sanjay?

He means well. When he says to Nancy, "I am a highly intelligent underachiever," that sums him up perfectly. I think he could do great things if he wanted: get good grades, get a good job, do what his parents want him to do. But it's not interesting to him. Instead he's decided, "I'm going to hang out with the pot dealers." He falls into it by accident through tutoring, when this hot mom asks him to do it [*laughs*]. There's something very scary and exciting about it, and obviously it's something he's never done before. In some ways he's easy to relate to because Sanjay's your average college kid, but he's just entered this whole new world and he's feeling his way through it. Everything he's doing is driven by impressing Nancy—he just wants to get her to smile at him once. The less attention she gives him, the more he wants it [*laughs*].

Sanjay's responsibilities bring new meaning to the term "grunt work"—pulling overnight shifts at the grow house and sticking his fingers up a dog's anus.

There is such joy in playing those scenes. Sanjay is so worried about messing up and everything goes wrong for him. Even in the first season, when he basically gets Nancy caught dealing on campus and then he turns up at the bakery to apologize to her—he brings her a basket full of cookies to a bakery! [*Laughs*] He's the youngest member of this group. Doug and Andy are in it for the pot, and he's in it for Nancy. It's fun to be on that journey with him as he tries to fit in with those guys, and with her.

What is the hardest part about being Sanjay?

To have to put yourself in the place of a guy who is so awkward and young. He gets dumped on [*laughs*]. Actually, I don't think it's *that* hard because he has such a persevering spirit. As difficult as it is emotionally for him to have to deal with not being part of the

group, he's like, "That's okay, I'll burn down the bakery." [*Laughs*] Everything rolls off of him, even when Conrad and Nancy find him cowering in the closet and yell at him on his cell phone.

Sanjay is a coward, though he starts to muster some courage by the end of the second season.

Sanjay's mantra for a while was "forgive me." He lives at home, he drives an old beat-up car, but once he gets some validation from the group, he starts coming into his own.

Director Craig Zisk says the grow house scenes often take a long time to shoot, so you must have an opportunity to get to know your castmates.

Yeah, those scenes generally involve Kevin Nealon, Justin, Romany, and Mary-Louise. Kevin is a comic genius. When you're hanging out with him on set, he'll say something hilarious, and then snicker as if he's surprised himself, like he didn't even know where the joke came from [*laughs*]. Mary-Louise is incredibly honest with wherever her character's at in the moment, so as soon as she's rolling, you just follow the scene with her because she goes there in such a profound way—she has this rare ability to startle you. Romany is so easy and fun, and you feel so relaxed with him. Justin is amazing—we had so many fun scenes together. It's kind of a motley crew. I've been on the show for two seasons now, it's such a great cast. Everybody is really excited about each other and their work. I feel so proud of every scene, every episode.

What were your favorite scenes to shoot?

In the first season, going in for that kiss with Nancy, and my face-off with Peter in the "fakery," where I was letting him know who was in charge [*laughs*]. I also loved the raid scene. It took a while to shoot—we actually had to shoot an extra day. It was kind of like sitting in a mini-action film. The grow house is four rooms, and we're running from room to room, tearing up plants. They had to reset the plants for the next shot and then we tore them up again. It was pretty involved. Justin and I had a lot of fun and the hours flew by. There was one scene from the raid that was cut where Andy and Sanjay run to the door, and Sanjay hyperventilates and Andy has to slap him [*laughs*].

The dog scene in the grow house was pretty brutal too.

It was insane. Justin had a boot on his foot, and on top of the boot was a little stuffed toy, and the dog had been trained to get the stuffed toy. The trainer held him on a leash, and the [crew] would show him the stuffed toy and get him all riled up, because they wanted him to spring out. But this dog was really salivating—he's a super-sweet dog, but he's ferocious looking, and he really became ferocious when he saw the stuffed toy [*laughs*]. There were a couple of times where I had to do the cheeseburger thing [*laughs*] and I would walk off and he would follow me. I was terrified that the dog was going to chase after me [*laughs*].

As a viewer, whom do you like to watch on the show?

I love Isabel. The whole Huskeroos thing, and seeing her dressed in lesbian gear—that stuff is outrageous. I love watching the scenes where Mary-Louise is really struggling with being a mom and grappling with who she is. Her scene with Romany where she smokes pot was so great to watch, and also her scene with Hunter on the lawn in front of Megan's house, when Mary-Louise put her hand over Megan's father's face. She's especially amazing when she's in that mode. For me, the joy of watching the show is seeing how these people deal with extraordinary circumstances that really aren't so crazy. Jenji says when she was growing up in suburbia, she had friends whose parents had tons of pot in their fridge. What I find so interesting about this series is that the show begins with a tragedy, and then opens the second season with Nancy's getting her business off the ground. But now everything has fallen apart. I can't wait to see where it goes from here.

In addition to his role as Sanjay, MAULIK PANCHOLY also plays Jonathan on NBC's *30 Rock*. Pancholy is in the forthcoming Mike Nichols' film *Charlie Wilson's War* with Tom Hanks, Philip Seymour Hoffman, and Julia Roberts. He has also appeared in the films *Friends with Money*, *Hitch*, *Good Sharma*, *Quarter Life Crisis*, *The Auteur Theory*, and the short film *Diwali*. He has had recurring roles on *The Comeback*, *Tracey Takes On*, and *Jack & Jill*, and guest roles on *Law & Order: Criminal Intent*, *The Sopranos*, *Charmed*, and *Felicity*.

Nancy Botwin's Contact Highs:
The Head of Distribution

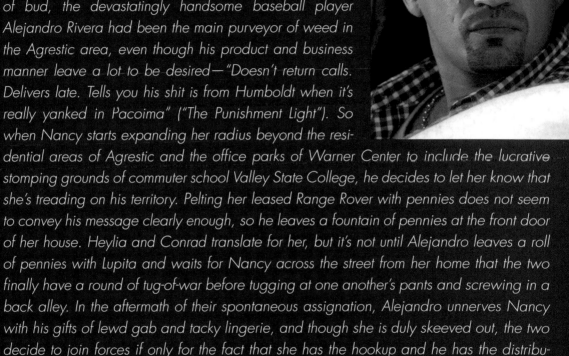

Alejandro Rivera,
played by Vincent Laresca

Before Nancy Botwin became the suburban baroness of bud, the devastatingly handsome baseball player Alejandro Rivera had been the main purveyor of weed in the Agrestic area, even though his product and business manner leave a lot to be desired—"Doesn't return calls. Delivers late. Tells you his shit is from Humboldt when it's really yanked in Pacoima" ("The Punishment Light"). So when Nancy starts expanding her radius beyond the residential areas of Agrestic and the office parks of Warner Center to include the lucrative stomping grounds of commuter school Valley State College, he decides to let her know that she's treading on his territory. Pelting her leased Range Rover with pennies does not seem to convey his message clearly enough, so he leaves a fountain of pennies at the front door of her house. Heylia and Conrad translate for her, but it's not until Alejandro leaves a roll of pennies with Lupita and waits for Nancy across the street from her home that the two finally have a round of tug-of-war before tugging at one another's pants and screwing in a back alley. In the aftermath of their spontaneous assignation, Alejandro unnerves Nancy with his gifts of lewd gab and tacky lingerie, and though she is duly skeeved out, the two decide to join forces if only for the fact that she has the hookup and he has the distribution connections. When Conrad and his plant temporarily part ways with Nancy and her team, Alejandro decides it's a good time to pursue his baseball career, leaving Agrestic for Toronto to train with the Blue Jays.

Vincent Laresca is a prolific television and film actor. He has most recently appeared in the films *Lords of Dogtown*, *Kiss Kiss Bang Bang*, and *The Aviator*, and has had recurring roles on *CSI: Miami* and *24*.

Heylia James's & Conrad Shepard's
Seven Habits of Highly Effective Pot Dealers

Heylia James is not merely the Rain Man of Weed. She's a shrewd and sagacious pot dealer who has steadily and cautiously grown her thriving, illicit business over a twenty-year period by heeding her own brand of ethics. Her nephew and middleman Conrad Shepard has recently defied his family by starting his own explosive grow business with Nancy Botwin. Both Heylia and Conrad have imparted bits of their wisdom to their reckless and naive protégée, including these seven indispensable lessons on being a successful purveyor of pot:

---

1. "You get what you ask for, child—and you never knew enough to ask for the call   brands. . . . Serious shit costs serious cash."

   (Heylia James, "Good Shit Lollipop")

2. "Only keep weed you know you're gonna move real quick at home."

   (Conrad Shepard, "Dead in the Nethers")

3. Build a secret locker. And you need to line that locker with cedar. Keeps the bugs away. . . . You protect your locker with a hidden lock. . . . The pot you're breaking into should be in a turkey bag. It hides the smell."

(Conrad Shepard, "Dead in the Nethers")

4. "Don't ever write anything down."

(Conrad Shepard, "Dead in the Nethers")

5. "The whole world don't need to know you've got the hookup or you're gonna be talking to your kids through a cage."

(Heylia James, "Higher Education")

6. "It's like a pyramid. You wanna be at the top. You've got people beneath you. And they've got soldiers beneath them, and those soldiers do not know you. And they damn well better not know me."

(Heylia James, "Higher Education")

7. "Fare's what you pay to ride the bus. That's the only fair I know."

(Heylia James, "The Godmother")

Aram Kesheshian,
Northside Armenian Power,
played by Arthur Darbinyan

Nancy and Conrad have unwittingly landed a grow house in the heart of the Northside Armenian Power territory. Drug lord Aram Kesheshian recognizes that he has new farmers moving in next door, by the familiar sight of boxes belonging to meth addict Victor, his own grow house contractor. Aram implores the newbies to leave at once, presenting them with a going-away present: a pink box filled with homemade baklava. But it's the mobsters who are on their way out when Nancy hands her husband Peter a map of the Armenian neighborhood; he delivers her a newly evacuated cul-de-sac after the DEA raids them and sends the gang to jail. When Peter turns against Nancy and Conrad, Heylia pays Aram a visit at the prison, commissioning him to set up a hit against the DEA agent with the money they expect to make from the sale of MILF Weed to U-Turn.

ARTHUR DARBINYAN has guest starred on the television series *Cold Case*, *Alias*, and *Thieves*.

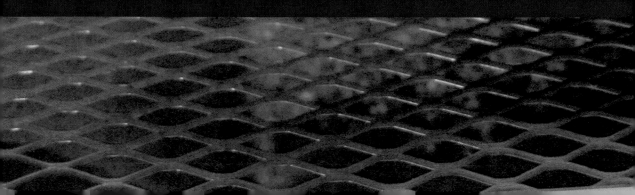

U-Turn, played by Page Kennedy

As likely to slice a piece of fruit for a friend as he is to take that knife and stab him for being disrespectful, U-Turn is the epitome of volatility. Once known as Louis, a kid who obliged his grandmother by dressing up in powder blue wide-lapeled suits and playing violin, now U-Turn is West Adams's most dangerous gangsta. Though she's not proud of it, Heylia had a hand in helping him set up his business, which provides her a necessary bargaining chip when she needs to learn the source of the hottest new strain on the streets. Only U-Turn has the courage to face Heylia's temper and rat out Conrad and Nancy.

There's something intriguing about a health-conscious, gun-toting thug who feasts on avocados (for the "good fat"), goes on maple lemonade fasts, and enjoys a good pedicure. But Conrad, who grew up with U-Turn in West Adams, knows enough to approach him with caution. His mistake is approaching him at all, even in his most desperate hour. Conrad initially comes to U-Turn after severing ties with Nancy, in pursuit of seed money for his grow business. But he quickly backs off and reunites with Nancy when he offers Conrad an unreasonable deal while hurling a knife at his posse for disrupting their business conversation. When Peter, Nancy's DEA husband, turns on them, Conrad is forced to go to U-Turn with a bargain basement offer on their last harvest: thirty-eight pounds for $300,000. The thug appears in the grow house kitchen armed with machine guns—his idea of a counter offer. "There ain't no money, fool. I'm a fucking criminal. Now open the safe 'fore I shoot all y'all!" ("Pittsburgh").

PAGE KENNEDY has guest starred on a number of television series, among them *The Shield, Six Feet Under, Desperate Housewives, Boston Legal, Pepper Dennis, CSI,* and the Showtime series *Barbershop.* He made his film debut as the villainous Travis Shipley in *S.W.A.T.,* supporting Samuel L. Jackson, Colin Farrell, Michelle Rodriguez, and LL Cool J.

BEHIND
THE SCENES:
Part Two

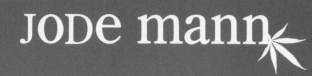

Budding Interests

A Conversation with Property Master

JODE mann

Weeds is a very prop-heavy show. What are your days like?

We make a lot of stuff, I rent some stuff, and I buy some stuff. I try to be on set at the opening of every scene, especially for heavy scenes, because the actors aren't involved in our pre-production meetings, and they may have a different notion of what they want to do in a scene. I work very closely with the actors. My assistants and I go over the schedule day by day. I have a bunch of bins in my office marked with every scene, and the props that go in them. It has to be really well choreographed. Every Monday I have the new script for the following week, and I try to get as much advance information as I can. This whole time we're shooting that week's episode and returning stuff from the previous episode. Tuesday I have a concept meeting with the set decorator, the construction coordinator, the art director, the producer, the director, and the assistant director, and go over the entire script in detail. I walk away from that and I'm pretty bitchy for the rest of the day [*laughs*] because I haven't quite fully completed the process of the episode I'm in, and I've just been inundated with more information. My mind is always spinning.

Do the actors come to you with ideas of what they want in their scenes?

Yes. Mary-Louise said early on, "I think my character should drink coffee." So we made contact with a coffee place out here [in L.A.] called It's A Grind. We have coffee for her nearly every time you see her. She comes up with props for her scenes a lot, and I suggest things, and we'll go back and forth.

That scene where she's sitting in the hallway outside of Silas's room, singing "Polly Wolly Doodle"—it was her idea to use a karaoke machine and all those instruments. The writers give the actors some room. The script will say, "Nancy is in the hallway singing," and then she can come up with more. Nancy is big on changing her sunglasses. We always forget about it and Mary-Louise will always ask for it. Elizabeth also comes to me in advance with things she'd like for a specific scene. She also likes sunglasses, and she really likes to have stuff in her hands.

Heylia is always making something in the kitchen. That must keep you busy.

Yes. Tonye is a very busy prop actress. When we'd have scenes at Heylia's, even a simple scene where Heylia is making dinner, you don't just have her making dinner—she's a serious cook. We had to hunt for kitchen gadgets every week [*laughs*]. Her rehearsals always included working with props. We practiced the sushi-rolling thing and the pasta-making machine—she didn't want it to look like it was the first time she was using the stuff. She wants to have things to do. We'd discuss these kinds of things in the content meetings, especially if a new director was coming in. I would tell them, "Tonye's going to want to be busy." That's one of the ways the show becomes a big collaboration: We're a link to the directors coming in every week, because we know the actors.

As a props master, you have probably bought or rented anything and everything in the world. So buying sex toys for Yael and Andy is just another day in your life?

[*Laughs*] Whenever you go into a sex shop and you say you're buying props for a TV show, there is usually this really large tattooed gay guy behind the counter, and he looks at you like, *Right.* But why would I need five dildos? [*Laughs*] I'm used to that kind of stuff—you get over your embarrassment pretty quickly. Now, presenting it to the actors is a whole other deal. When I saw Justin, I was like, "I got a present for you today [*laughs*].

I brought you these four dildos." Then I had to try to get them through the ring [of the strap-on harness]. I've never used one, and seeing as these guys have penises, I said to the director and the crew, "You guys try putting it in there." I didn't want to hurt it [laughs].

The scene where Andy gets his toes bitten off by Mr. Sweaters, the Armenians' pit bull, looked extremely complicated to pull off, as it were.

Yeah, there was the issue of the dog, with the gold necklace and finding the kind of burgers we could have around there. I had to use fake burgers and real burgers, because too much food will distract the dog—if you want an animal to do a certain thing, they're not going to resist a new burger; I don't care how well trained they are. Then there is the foot: We had to make a prosthetic foot, which was what you saw when the dog was pulling on the foot. The wardrobe people came and worked with the prosthetic to create a fake boot that Justin wore when the dog was tugging at it for a shot from another angle. Then we had the green screen, and we had to get some chroma-key paint and paint out his toes. That little five-second scene was extraordinarily expensive.

What kinds of props do you make?

We made about twenty pounds of pot—all the pot you saw in the safe. We came up with a really good combination this year. I got some wood dowels and cut them down to different lengths. Then we combined hot glue, parsley, oregano, some Mexican seasonings, and kosher salt in a huge mixing bowl. I mix it all up until I get the texture and the look that I want. I had two people on it for three days straight making all of it. You get all different sizes and shapes of little buds and bigger buds. We also made all the roots for the plants that were pulled up during the drug bust, when Sanjay and Andy pull up all the plants and try to flush them down the toilet. The fake plants only have a stem, so I found some other weird plants that have roots and we attached them. I also did the campaign stuff for Celia, all the signs, and I came up with the buttons. Celia is a fun character for me, and Elizabeth is very appreciative of all of it.

Justin says that he and Kevin are getting a buzz off that herbal concoction they're smoking on the set. What are you packing in their peace pipes?

[*Laughs*] It's a problem, and we explain this to everyone who smokes any of our "pot." We use honey rose cigarettes, which are non-nicotine cigarettes, and they're actually hard to get. If you don't smoke, it's gonna give you a buzz. The first episode Justin was on, he got so stoned because he had to take so many bong hits in his scene. I couldn't use a vaporizer. Justin and Kevin are the most easygoing guys.

Your job is extremely hectic by nature. What have been some of your most challenging tasks?

The biggest challenges are usually the easiest things. I spent a tremendous amount of time on the Mohasky Cup, rigging the vaporizer so that it could work on command, and all the other pipes and pot samplings. It looked great and it was awesome but it was exhausting. Set dressing did an amazing job and then we filled it in. The mayhem in the grow house bust was really hard too, because we had to clean up the mess, and then put it all back together again exactly as it was so we could do another take. There are certain things that are always difficult, and then you find the right thing and you forget about it, like childbirth [*laughs*]. I think the hardest thing to come up with this season was figuring out how to make Doug's drool for his fight with Dean [in the second season finale]. When I read that detail in the script, I thought, "Kevin could do this." But Kevin said, "Believe it or not, spitting was the one thing I was never good at." My poor assistant, Hardy, must have tried twenty different things in his mouth. I said, "Try toothpaste mixed with orange juice. Try peanut butter." He just looked at me like, *I hate you so much!* He was so nauseous. We ended up with egg whites. The stupidest little thing and it gave me such a run for my money [*laughs*].

How to Build a Fake Grow House
A Conversation with Set Decorator
Julie Bolder

The producers may have to use fake weed on the series, (see "Budding Interests: A Conversation with Property Master Jode Mann"), but they were determined to have a real grow house built for Nancy, Conrad, and the gang during the second season. As Set Decorator Julie Bolder explains, it's far from easy to be green.

Where do you even begin with a project like this?

There was a lot of research. I had a technical advisor, Mike Straumietis from Advanced Nutrients, who provided the equipment and shipped it out of Canada. He had to teach me and my crew how to do it. The producers didn't just want it to look good and be shootable—they required it be technically correct so that viewers who know how a grow house functions would believe it. We never want anyone saying, "That's not how they do that!"

What kinds of things did you have to learn?

Everything about lighting, hydroponic nutrients, timers, how many plants per light, how it's done,

and how many turnovers you have in a year for marijuana. It was an incredible amount of detail, and all that had to be done in an incredibly short amount of time. I think one of the reasons we have such a big following is because we pay such close attention to detail, and we know what we're talking about.

You probably learned as much as Nancy and Conrad! Property Master Jode Mann said all of the fake pot plants were made for the show. Where did you get those?

Yes, all the pot in the grow house had to be custom made because Jenji wanted it magical. They were made for us by a small Florida-based company called New Image Plants. We went back and forth with the manufacturer with pictures, saying we want these kinds of buds—because there are a lot of different kinds of buds out there—and we wanted this leaf shape, and this size, etc. Of course we had no time, as usual, and they were like, "We can't do it that fast!" But somehow they did it! They geared up a whole operation and made a big truckload—a semi!—of fake marijuana plants. It was so hysterical because they unloaded the shipment on Cahuenga Boulevard in Hollywood, these big pallets of pot plants. It gave me the chills. I took all these pictures, and was expecting the cops to show up any minute. I wished they had, actually. New Image Plants actually makes these plants for police academies to train new recruits, show them what pot plants look like. After we ordered a *massive* amount of plants, we kind of put this company on the map. I talked to an AP reporter who was doing a feature about the sudden growth of New Image Plants, and the article ended up being in papers around the world. There were a lot of people out there making fake marijuana, but this company is the only one whose plants look really real.

What makes them more real-looking?

They're made out of silk, and they custom made all of them for us. Then our paint department added color to the buds, because some buds have purple tones, some have green tones, etc. We also added crystals, because real buds glisten in the light, and have shiny trichomes on them. Jenji wanted to be *that* accurate—she has a big book of bud. Jenji has done a very good job of representing things accurately. And we studied those pictures very closely. We had great resources—our guy at Advanced Nutrients, plus *High Times*, NORML, *Cannabis Culture* magazine, Marijuana Policy Project, practically everyone in the "industry."

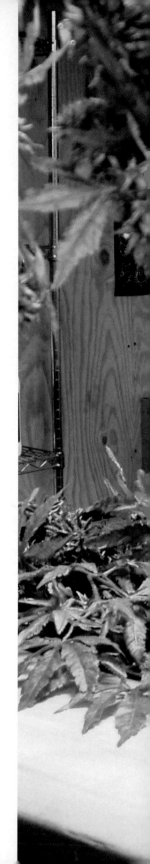

aGrestic: THE BEST OF THE BEST-IC

The Pursuit of the Mythic Suburb

Agrestic is the private southern California community that is home to the Botwins, the Hodeses, and the Wilsons. McMansion-like tract houses on the hillside may be as ubiquitous as SUVs and Starbucks, but creating a fictional suburb proved to be a bit more challenging. Jenji Kohan, Location Manager Paul Boydston, Line Producer Mark Burley, and Set Decorator Julie Bolder recount their quest for Agrestic, and Elizabeth Perkins and Story Editor Rolin Jones describe the neighborhoods that may have inspired them.

How did you find the place that would become Agrestic?

JENJI: The tech scouts introduced me to these places. We'd load up in a big, white nine-person passenger van. We were going all over to suburban communities in the outskirts of L.A. Sometimes we'd have appointments at houses, but other times we'd drop by places because we liked the landscape and the look of the house. We'd just go knock on the door, and inevitably there would be a woman there, home alone, and she'd invite nine strangers from a white van into her air-conditioned house and show us how she decorated her home, and talk about living there. It happened over and over. It was absolutely fascinating and crazy: These people are living there all alone in the air-conditioning, not talking to each other. Every home had all the decorating magazines—these people all decorate, and very often they've blown their wad on the living room, so it's fully done and then there's like a card table in the dining room because the new dining room table hadn't come in yet, or they ran out of money. The kitchen is the center of the household, where everyone hangs out, and it opens out onto the family room, just like Nancy's. And they always had these wooden butlers holding out a sign [*laughs*]. The kids' rooms are totally

194

done up—those were over the top—even if the adults' room hadn't been done yet. I hadn't spent a whole lot of time in Agrestic-like communities before the show. It was amazing to be able to walk into these people's homes and walk into their lives like that.

PAUL BOYDSTON: Jenji popped Malvina Reynolds's "Little Boxes" into the van's CD player and said, "Guys, I'm thinking of this." So Mark Burley, Jenji, and I spent a lot of time running around, looking at various neighborhoods, because Jenji wanted to create that new—but not "dirt-yard new"—neighborhood on the edge of L.A., an upscale nouveau riche, new tract house development.

Where is Agrestic?

PAUL: We shoot our exterior shots primarily in an area called Stevenson Ranch in the Santa Clarita Valley, which is over the hill, north of L.A., off the I-5. It's near the Magic Mountain theme park. It's the one location we travel to on a regular basis that's far from Ren-Mar Studios in L.A., where we shoot the show. When the show was green-lighted, Mark said all of our locations, with the exception of the neighborhood, had to be within a block of the studio [laughs]. "Look around you," Mark said, "and don't look past a block." We have done a lot of filming in Stevenson Ranch because it looks so cool and we've gotten such a positive response. But because we were filming there a lot, we started getting complaints from neighbors, so we are

looking around for a similar neighborhood to give these guys a break. I mean, it may have been exciting for this community the first ten or fifteen times we were there, but with all the trucks and cameras and people blocking streets and driveways, it stops being interesting. Recently I spent a whole week looking for a similar neighborhood. The development is slightly newer, and the houses are a tad smaller, but I don't think they'd look that way on film. The floor plans and layouts are the same, and we even found some backup streets that look enough like the places we've been using. So we've been able to give our primary neighborhood a bit of relief by filming some other scenes in what I like to call our "mirror neighborhood."

Where can we find West Adams, Heylia James's neighborhood?

PAUL: West Adams references South Central L.A., an area that begins just as you cross the 10 freeway heading south out of Hollywood. The houses there are typically built in a craftsman bungalow style. We were lucky enough to find three or four houses a block from the studio to use for the exterior shots, that were made in that architectural style.

Are all of the interiors shot in Ren-Mar Studios?

MARK BURLEY: Most of them. The four main stages and sets include Nancy's house, which has a downstairs and an upstairs—those are two separate pieces joined together; the Hodes house; Heylia's house; and Doug's office. They are all on one big stage called Stage 8 and 9. In the first season we had the bakery as a set and some swing sets [sets that convert into other rooms]. Second season we had the grow house on Stage 6. We converted the bakery into the rabbinical school. All of our sets are on two stages in the same studio.

JULIE BOLDER: We rework sets that we already have. Silas's bedroom also converts into Andy's bedroom, and it has probably been a couple other things besides that. We take the same room, and in a couple of days, the production designer Joseph Lucky will have his guys come in and repaint, and maybe even make some architectural changes. In the first season there were weeks where we needed to make fifteen swing sets in five days. We actually converted Roberto Benabib's office into the medical marijuana clinic. We took everything out of his office, brought in a whole clinic, and set it up, shot it, and then restored his office. The "fakery" had been the Indian restaurant, the rabbinical school—both the classroom and Yael's office, just redressed.

MARK: We also got more bang for our buck in the neighborhood: There are two buildings right next door to the studios, which we've used as locations. One is the Boys & Girls Club of Hollywood. All the scenes that are in the school corridors and classrooms are shot there. We started using it in the first season and they were very helpful. Then, across the road, the musicians' union has various things in there. We started using it for the city council meeting, the debate scene, and the election scene, the lobby for when Dean got fired; we turned the basement into a shooting range for Nancy and Peter. They've been very helpful.

Are there places in southern California that you think serve as the inspiration for Agrestic?

ELIZABETH PERKINS: There is a community out here called Valencia, and it's growing at such an astounding rate. They built a Main Street area, and made it crooked on purpose so that it looked like it moved a little. Then they did faux antiquing on the buildings so it looked like they'd been there for a while. It's like we're living in Disneyland, established in 2005 [*laughs*]. That's why I love what Jenji's doing, because she's making such a statement about suburbia and how we're just fighting tooth and nail for this unreal existence. I mean, we're fighting a war in Iraq to protect this American dream that's just a big phony lie. And yet underneath the pristine facade, there's this grotesqueness: the pot, which is metaphorical for the dirty underbelly. This has been a real learning process for me. I mean, we drive out to places that I can't even believe exist.

We're talking little boxes on the hillside, literally. And every week we go, there is another row, and another row, and another row, and they all look exactly the same. I just moved to a brand-new house. It's the first time I've lived in a brand-new house in my entire life. There's a feeling of soullessness to it, of prefab, and transience, like it's not really grounded and not really real. That's the feeling you get when you go out to these suburbs like Agrestic. You feel like there aren't really people living in the houses—it doesn't feel like a home; it feels like a house. You've got people living in them who don't feel grounded themselves. I can never imagine living in a place like Agrestic, which is what makes this fun for me.

PAUL: I think the beauty of what Jenji and Mark ended up with when they picked that neighborhood—and what they sort of fell in love with—was, not only was it what Jenji was imagining, but [it was] the result of what she was imagining. Now, I don't think there's a person who can watch it who doesn't say, "I know that neighborhood." Because it looks like and gives off the feel of some neighborhood that someone can identify with. Now that the show is known, we'll go into neighborhoods, knock on doors, and talk to people, and somebody will pull you in the door a little bit, and whisper, "You know, there's a lady down the street who sells pot. You're not making this stuff up." Does life imitate art or art imitate life?

ROLIN JONES: I grew up in the San Fernando Valley, in Woodland Hills. I wasn't up in the hills where these subdivisions are, but I went to school with people like that, and I went over to their houses. When I am assigned an episode, and even before each season, I take a nighttime walk around what I consider my personal Agrestic, which is right near Bell Canyon. It's this little place slammed up against these desert rocks. I go there just to get in touch, and to see if there is anything else out there that we could re-create—a mood or an atmosphere. They're such interesting communities, because they're preplanned, but they are put up against wild, unkempt, untouched properties. So the mountain lion lives right outside the neighborhood, and at night there's something weird that happens when the Santa Ana desert winds come in. It's a very, very specific place.

The Sound of Grass Growing
The Music of *Weeds*

Jenji and her husband, the writer Christopher Noxon, boast a catalog-like knowledge of music with an eclectic library to match. Joining forces with music supervisor and KCRW DJ Gary Calamar, they have assembled a carefully considered soundtrack that strikes all of Weeds's poignant chords, from its winsome, often irreverent humor, to its dark, affecting drama. In the second season, they recruited composers Gwendolyn Sanford and Brandon Young Jay to create a score and enliven the Agrestic hills with the sound of music. (For a complete song list, go to "The Weeds Playlist.")

Your husband is an author (his book, *Rejuvenile,* makes several cameos in the series) who served as the informal music supervisor during the first season. How did he come to contribute to the soundtrack?

JENJI: Chris and I are obsessed with music. During the pilot we happened to be editing in the same building where my husband had an office, and when we needed music, I would go to him. He grabbed the CDs out of the car and burned stuff off of iTunes [*laughs*]. He got really involved with the music for the pilot. We had hired another music supervisor, but Chris was even better. But by second season, he was too busy to do it.

There are a lot of music aficionados working on the show—producers, writers, cast members. Does everybody weigh in?

GARY CALAMAR: All of the people on the show are very music savvy, so yeah, it's a huge collaboration. When I came on for the second season, I began by giving Jenji and Mark Burley quite a bit of music that I thought fit the vibe of the show and our budget. They keep that as a bank, and when the editors do their thing, they sometimes go to the folder of music that I sent. I might have a folder for Nancy music, one for Silas, etc. But I don't make any final decisions on this particular show. I'm like the waiter in a fine restaurant, bringing choices for them, pitching them songs, and it's a group decision determining what works. If Jenji loves something, we'll find a way to make that work.

Where do you even begin?

GARY: *Weeds* has a very modest budget, so that narrows the playing field right off the bat, but fortunately a lot of cool artists like the show a lot, so many times they'll want to work with us. Some artists are thrilled to do it for the exposure, especially now that the Showtime website features the songs: The music is streamed in, and the website tells you how to get in touch with the artist. So it is helpful, and in fact it makes my job easier to know my boundaries and restrictions. If we're way over budget, we'll go to our composers, Gwendolyn and Brandon, and see if they can do some piano music in the background at a bar, for example.

The song "I Can't Move," which appears in the first season with a constipated Celia on the toilet, couldn't be more perfect. Where do you find the rare gems that turn up on the soundtrack?

JENJI: Chris is in a CD club with his friends, where they send one another mixes every few weeks, and "I Can't Move" was playing at an installation at an art show. The guy wasn't even a musician—he'd written it for his installation. We had to track him down. It was Mark Burley's idea to match that song up with the scene. It's the gift of a creative line producer who can see that. It was perfect. Very often when we're writing, the writers will include music. Rolin always writes in what music he wants. He's a huge Sufjan Stevens and Regina Spektor fan.

Since becoming the music supervisor, what are some of your favorite songs on the second season soundtrack?

GARY: Jenny Owen Youngs, who did "Fuck Was I." She's an indie artist who is just starting to get a little bit of attention. I've been a fan of hers, playing her on the radio, and I was thrilled the *Weeds* people liked her. Also the group Zeroleen's "All Good," which we used for the growing montage. We've embraced it as our song.

Whose idea was it to have different artists cover "Little Boxes"?

MARK BURLEY: It was an idea I proposed early on. Jenji had written the song into the pilot script, but we weren't sure if we were going to get to use Malvina Reynolds's version for licensing reasons, so we asked some local artists to do a version. In the end we got to use Malvina's. But we all got really into the idea of using different artists, so we decided to do it for season two.

GARY: Because we had a modest budget, we had to call in favors from fans of the show. Mary-Louise is friends with Elvis Costello—he was traveling in Japan and did his recording in a church. Death Cab for Cutie are friends of mine. Regina Spektor did one too, in part because Rolin Jones had written one of her songs, "Ghost of Corporate Future," into an episode as a score. She's on a major label and publisher, but they did us a special favor because of the way he'd structured the episode around her song.

In the second season, the producers brought in Gwendolyn Sanford and Brandon Young Jay to compose original music for the show. How did you discover them?

JENJI: They had fronted a kids band that my kids love, called Gwendolyn and the Good Time Gang. The two of them turned out to be the most talented composers I've ever met in my life. They are so energetic, so on top of it, so ahead of the game, and they so get the show. They were up against Stewart Copeland and really heavyweight composers, and they blew them all away. I think they brought a cohesiveness and a sound to the show, tying it together in a way that we didn't have the first season.

GARY: They really hit a home run with their score. Gwendolyn and Brandon are both pretty well known in and around Los Angeles. Gwendolyn is very quirky and cool in all of her musical ventures, and so is Brandon. He used to play in this band called The 88, and now has a band called Quazar and the Bamboozled. Their music really adds to the whole texture of the show.

Gwendolyn and Brandon, have you ever scored a television show before?

GWENDOLYN: No. It was a big learning experience. We were kind of scrambling to figure out how all of it works in those first couple of episodes. I did a small film for

someone on a lark about one and a half years ago, but it's very different when you only have three or four days. Once we signed on, we gave them forty to fifty cues before they even started plugging in the music—we got inspired, and decided that the library was the way to go to make the spotting sessions so much easier.

BRANDON: Sometimes we'll try a couple of different cues or pieces for a scene to give them different options.

How do the music responsibilities break down, orchestrally speaking?

GWENDOLYN: Brandon and I do more of the signature sound with the guitar, percussion, and the main piano, like the piece "From Agrestic to Las Vegas," where Nancy is flying to Vegas with Peter. Our friend Ryan "Shmedly" Maynes is a keyboard player, and we turn to him for a lot of source music. He's a big TV fan—his brain is like a big library. If we need strings, Shmedly helps us orchestrate the cue because he's got all of these different samples in his keyboard, like tablas and sitars. He's also a genius at background music—he did the game show sounds at U-Turn's house. And he's really good at "smooth jazz," and loves to parody stuff.

BRANDON: Our friend Robert Petersen is our hip-hop go-to guy. He helped us with Snoop Dogg, and the background gangsta music at U-Turn's house.

You bring out the show's winsome nature, as with your piece "Shane Digs Gretchen," which plays as he stares at her dreamily before kicking her in front of her locker, and "From Agrestic to Las Vegas."

GWENDOLYN: There's always an upside to *Weeds*, which we try to magnify, because when dark spots come, boy do they come. Despite those dark twisty spots, Nancy always feels like she's going to get herself out of it.

The editors took one of your children's songs, "Little Monkey," and used it in a sex scene between Silas and Megan. That must have taken you by surprise.

GWENDOLYN: I fell out of my bed when I watched the episode [*laughs*]. But it fit so well into that scene with Silas and Megan, and when they asked us if they could use it for that, well, I just didn't have the heart to say no [*laughs*].

BRANDON: Jenji and Chris told us that they were watching the episode, and their children, who are big fans of Gwendolyn and the Good Time Gang, were in the other room. They came running in yelling, "*Oh, Gwendolyn!*" And [Jenji and Chris] were like, "NO, NO, NO!" We couldn't believe it when we saw it.

GWENDOLYN: And then my mother saw it [*laughs*]. I had just come to grips with it and then the embarrassment set in all over again. She was like, "*Gwendolyn, that's your song!*" [*Laughs*] One time, when we were sitting in a spotting session [cuing the music to the scenes], Jenji looked over at me and said, "We're all going to hell." I have a lot of great little fans, and I really hope they're not watching *Weeds*.

In the Weeds with

CELIA HODES:

Mrs. Mid-level Asshole

THE DOPE ON . . .
CELIA

Celia Hodes may be the biggest bitch in Agrestic — and its most notorious voyeur — but everything in her life has fallen far below her impossible expectations. After sixteen years of marriage, Celia believes she has become "Mrs. Mid-level Asshole," settling into a life of bourgeois mediocrity. She lives with her family of four in the "ridiculous house" (with a "stupid atrium where plants come to die") that her husband, Dean, got a "great deal" on, in an upper-middle-class community comprising uniformly designed homes

HODES

("The Punishment Light"). And they're not upgrading anytime soon: Dean has not only been passed over for a partnership at his law firm; he's been fired and then Tasered on his way out the door. Their marriage is just barely surviving, especially after Dean's indiscreet affair at their country club with Helen Chin (played by Michelle Krusiec), the cute Asian tennis instructor who sticks a racquet up his ass. Celia's daughters, Quinn (see "Celia Hodes's Kif and Kin: The Older Daughter: Quinn Hodes") and Isabel, refuse to offer any consolation; after years of being antagonized by their mother, the two girls live to spite, spite to live. But if there's one thing Celia can't bear, it's facing her harsh reality. "I don't like dealing with things," she tells Helen. "I'd much prefer to pretend they don't exist" ("Free Goat").

Had she not been born to her fastidious, narcissistic, church-lady mother, Pat (played by Concetta Tomei)—who reserves all affection and altruistic gestures for her fellow congregants, especially Mr. Daniels, "the cripple" with the "unusually large head" ("Higher Education")—contentment might have been within Celia's grasp. But she adopts the kind of ruthless tactics and tenets by which her mother abided, subsequently earning her daughters' scorn. She reads Quinn's diary and uses a nanny-cam cloaked in a pink teddy bear to monitor young Isabel's eating habits and Quinn's sexual interactions with her boyfriend, Silas Botwin. "[Kids] are all liars and sneaks and it is our job to discover what they're up to and stop it," Celia tells Nancy Botwin. "I don't want Quinn turning into some little slut like that deaf girl down on Dewey Street who gave fellatio to Dennis Kling" ("You Can't Miss the Bear").

But chutzpah begets chutzpah: Quinn turns the nanny-cam intended for her and Silas on her father and the tennis pro, capturing them in the act, and ensuring that her mother will screen it. Celia not only gets the surprise footage of Dean being impaled by a tennis racquet while *shtupping* another woman; she also gets a bonus shot of smug Quinn flicking her middle fingers in the air, mouthing, "Fuck you!" and reveling in the schadenfreude. "That little cunt," Celia mutters. "I should have had an abortion" (`You Can't Miss the Bear'). Since it's more than fifteen years too late for that, she does what she perceives to be the next best thing: Celia ships Quinn off to a Mexican boarding school. But the girl doesn't flinch; Quinn spends her last forty-eight hours at home dying her hair and loading thousands of songs onto her iPod. Once she's in Mexico, she refuses to return home, even when Celia gets a "touch of the [breast] cancer" ("The Punishment Lighter").

Isabel is not as jaded as Quinn, but she does become less forgiving after learning that Celia is the bowelless culprit behind her gruesome diarrhea explosion in art class, having switched out her secret stash of chocolates for Ex-Lax. Celia confesses to Dean, "[Isabel]

shit herself because she's a little piggy," rationalizing that "shit girl is better than being called fat girl" ("Good Shit Lollipop"). Taking a page from Quinn's book of vengeance, Isabel swaps her mother's Trim-Spa diet pills for Imodium AD tablets, stopping up her mother for days. Isabel really sticks it to Celia when she tries to keep her from pursuing what turns out to be an incredibly lucrative modeling career for Huskeroos—the clothing line for larger kids. She hires CPA Doug Wilson—Celia's archenemy—as her financial advisor; appoints Dean as her manager; and cuts Mom out of everything.

Celia is poised for a total transformation after a cargo plane crashes into their home, and cancer cells rob her of her breasts. But before she has a mastectomy, she has a little acting out to do. She begins by giving her "puppies" a proper send-off. "I'm really gonna miss my babies," Celia laments

over martinis with Nancy. "[My breasts and I] had some good times together." She drunkenly flashes them at Silas, which enrages his mother. "I just wanted to show my breasts to someone who would appreciate them. . . . Sorry. I took a 'lude" ("'Lude Awakening"). Celia decides to commemorate them with a tattoo—"Here Today, Gone Tomorrow"—on her left breast ("My homage to temporary permanence" ("Dead in the Nethers"), and, as a finale, gets "nailed" by Nancy's "carpenter," Conrad, after the three go nightclubbing.

Celia sleeps with Conrad, not only to get back at Dean, but also as an attempt to bond with Nancy, her mysteriously well off, widowed neighbor, fellow PTA mom, and, to Celia's mind, the only interesting S in Agrestic. Exasperated with Dean, and hopelessly fixated on Nancy, Celia jokingly contemplates her sexuality with her before their night on the town: "I'm sick of men," she kvetches. "What if I missed my calling? Maybe I was supposed to be a dyke and took a wrong turn by mistake. That would explain a hell of a lot" ("Good Shit Lollipop"). The longer the two women are acquainted, the less Celia feels she knows her emotionally elusive pal. For a woman who once boasted that "there are no secrets in this town" ("Free Goat"), it is ironic that Celia remains the only person in Agrestic who isn't apprised of Nancy's business, especially since Dean is one of her best clients *and* a partner in crime.

Celia confesses her retaliatory affair to Dean right away, and gives away all of her clothes and most of their furniture to their house cleaner, Blanca (played by Soledad St. Hilaire). Despite her bad behavior, he forgives Celia everything. Both he and Isabel yearn for her love, and he gladly goes on double-cheeseburger runs and accompanies Celia on her chemotherapy treatments, while Isabel cautiously embraces her mother's affectionate overtures. A surprise visit in the hospital by Celia's appearance-obsessed

mother renders her even more vulnerable, and she exposes her potential for humanity as she attempts to reach out to her mother, revealing the insights she has gleaned from catharsis. "[My cancer comes] from an irregular cell on a mission. This cancer is almost like a weird blessing," she tells Pat, who dismisses her observation with disgust ("Higher Education"). When Celia returns home from the hospital, Pat tears through their household, demeaning her husband and daughter until finally, Celia rebukes her—"We're tired of you working out your psychotic bullshit on the family" ("Higher Education")—and Dean kicks her out, bringing the family closer together than ever before. But the bond lasts only as long as Celia's treatment. Once she starts wearing her new, platinum blond Marilyn Monroe wig, Celia emerges stronger and more brazen than ever before, which Isabel discovers during a steamy playdate with her friend Peggy Lee (see "Isabel Hodes's Special Bud: Peggy Lee") (played by Olivia Sui).

At least Agrestic provides a couple of outlets for Celia's power hunger. Though her breast cancer diagnosis temporarily sidelines her, Celia reigns as the formidable president of the PTA, lording over Maggie Reynolds, Alison Alderson (see "Celia Hodes's Fronds Indeed: The Hypo-Christian Bitch Moms") (played by Tressa DiFiglia and Shawn Schepps), and Pam Gruber—the "hypo-Christian bitch moms," as Nancy dubs them ("Fashion of the Christ"). The Eve Harrington–like Maggie attempts to launch a coup d'etat—"We need a reliable and healthy leader" ("The Punishment Lighter")—but her plan backfires, big time. Celia not only recovers her presidency, but proudly informs Maggie that the school districts are being redrawn, disqualifying her membership in the Agrestic PTA. Empowered by her blond wig; her hopelessly devoted charge, Pam; and Nancy's throwaway joke that she takes as a genuine suggestion, Celia sets her sights on Doug Wilson's city council seat when he ignores her plea for a traffic light at the intersection where she got into a car accident. She feels totally justified after the "fuckhead" ("Corn Snake") humiliates her in a town meeting. But Doug relies on his stature as "City Councilman Doug," the unopposed candidate, and promotes her from a "raging bitch" ("You Can't Miss the Bear") to "cancer cunt" ("Cooking with Jesus") for threatening to take that away from him.

Celia's run for office brings her entire life to a crisis point. She rejects Dean's offer to serve as her campaign manager, and instead enlists Pam, her fiercely loyal, idiot friend-by-default. Celia is left posing with only her neighbor's yipping Chihuahua for her family values campaign poster when Dean stomps out of the house and Isabel refuses to comply with her request to change out of her Willie Nelson–esque baby dyke outfit. What's worse, her recently fired lawyer-husband signs on to help Doug with *his* campaign.

More desperate than ever for her friendship, Celia uses the upcoming election as a pretext to determine Nancy's loyalty to her, badgering her for help with her campaign—with lukewarm results. Nancy's increasing inaccessibility rankles her, not least of all because Celia worries she'll forever be stuck with Pam. She interprets Nancy's distraction as ambivalence and disinterest in their friendship. If Nancy would just indulge her demand for affirmation, Celia's neediness might subside. She can't bear the uncertainty anymore, and puts everything on the line. "I tell you about my husband's unemployment, my daughter being the face of American trans fat. So tell me what's going on with you. Please, Nancy. Aren't we friends? . . . You can't even say it. You don't want to be my friend." Nancy recoils at confrontation, inadvertently detonating Celia's explosive temper. She pulls Nancy's hair, yelling, "BE MY FRIEND! BE MY FRIEND! SELFISH! SELFISH! SELFISH!" ("Mrs. Botwin's Neighborhood").

At least Celia wins the election, if only by a fluke, when Dean forgets to file the papers that would put Doug's name on the ballot, which costs him Doug's friendship, yet fails to earn him his wife's gratitude. But city council isn't as easy to negotiate as Celia imagined. Bored and sexually neglected by his pole-dancing wife, Dana, Doug turns up at the town meetings out of habit, and finds himself counseling a warily appreciative Celia on the intricacies of Agrestic politics. Much to their surprise, advice proves to be a potent aphrodisiac: The two delve into a hot-and-heavy love affair as Celia is simultaneously launching her aggressive antidrug campaign by installing surveillance cameras all over town. During their assignations,

the two raptly watch the suburban soft-porn-like videos, which include footage of a neighbor defecating in a manhole, an anorexic woman speed-walking, and naked Mr. Lippman riding his Segway. But their entertainment is threatened when a thief starts stealing the cameras and the DRUG-FREE ZONE signs. Celia embarks on a quest to find out who is depriving her of their voyeuristic sustenance.

As the trysts become more frequent and intense, Celia tells Doug she's willing to divorce Dean if he'll leave Dana. Celia divulges her plan to an incredulous Dean. "Doug hates you," he says. "He loves me now," quips Celia ("Yeah. Like Tomatoes"). But Doug doesn't hold up his end of the bargain. He tells Celia, "You know, Dean used to talk about the terrible things you'd say to him. The horrible way you'd treat him. Dana won't fuck me, but she's a sweetheart. It's nice to live with sweet. You're not sweet" ("Yeah. Like Tomatoes"). Devastated and dejected, Celia drags herself home, ready to reassume her place in the household, only to find Dean lining up packed suitcases by the front door. "Stop being such a drama queen," she says. "You're not going anywhere. Neither am I." But he tells her he's "done," as he tosses her out with her bags and car keys. "Just my luck. Fucking loser finally grows a sack," she says ("Yeah. Like Tomatoes").

Homeless, friendless, abandoned by her family, and flying off the rails, Celia ramps up her pursuit of the surveillance-camera bandit and discovers, with great pleasure, that it is Silas. Now she just needs to track him down. With nothing more to lose, Celia blazes through Nancy's kitchen, brandishing a handgun she has borrowed from Pam, and, shocking everyone including herself, blows a hole through her cupboard. "Oh my God, that was my only bullet," she exclaims. "I was gonna shoot Doug. See you at graduation" ("Pittsburgh"). Together with a police officer, she finds Silas and has him arrested for the petty crime, one that is about to snowball into something far larger than she could have possibly imagined: The trunk of his car is loaded with hundreds of thousands of dollars' worth of MILF Weed. Celia finally has something to hold over Nancy's head—if only she knew how much and what to do with it.

Celia Hodes isn't the easiest person in the world to love—she terrorizes her family, the PTA, and the town of Agrestic, and now she's alienated Nancy Botwin. What did you make of her when you read the pilot script?

I fell in love with Celia immediately. *Immediately.* On the written page, Celia may come off as two-dimensional, but when you really start exploring her character after the second or third script, there is an enormous vulnerability to her. She's so over the top and bizarre—I've never seen another character like her before. You don't get to find that three-dimensional character very often. You usually just get the town bitch, and it doesn't get to go any further. But there is so much nuance, and Jenji allows me moments when Celia really falls—you really see the pain that she's in. It's really challenging for me to play Celia, and I just jumped at the opportunity. I'm really glad I'm playing Celia. I'm having a ball. It's funny, one of the first things I asked Jenji the first time I met her was, "Is this a comedy or a drama?" She said, "It's a comedy. Why? Do you think it's a drama?" I said, "I don't know, is it?" It's hard. At first viewing, the show appears to be this outrageous comedy, but if you really listen for it, the writers are making some serious social commentaries. And if you're looking more for that, you'll get more out of the show. There isn't, "Oh, here's that learning moment." It happens subtly, so that you don't feel like you're being preached to. There is no moral lesson that's being taught. It's only the moral experiences of the characters.

Do you like Celia?

I love Celia. I love her viewpoint on the world. She just tells it like it is. Like when she goes over to Nancy's house and Nancy is clearly not going to help her with the city council campaign, and she says, "So, you're just not going to help me, are you?" Most people would just beat around the bush. Nancy is so uncomfortable with confrontation, and that's why there's always that weird tension between the two of them. Or, in another instance,

Celia goes to her house and tells her, "I want to have sex with a woman because I'm sick of sucking dick." I don't know anybody who would come into a room and say that. Well, except probably my best friend [*laughs*]. I think deep down inside, Celia Hodes could be one of the great women of the world, but she's the victim of her own circumstances and consequently has sort of turned into this horror show. Underneath it all there is this great, bright, ambitious, sexy, smart woman who just has no outlet and no place to go. What's her outlet? The PTA? The city council? In a lot of ways Agrestic is a little bit beneath her and she's had to crouch just to stay in that community. It's difficult for her to crouch, so every now and then she stands up; and every time she stands up, she falls down . . . so she goes back to crouching. If she could just earn the trust of somebody, she would probably be the most loyal, committed friend, mother, wife you could possibly have. She just has no trust in anybody because everybody turns on her. Every once in a while Jenji gives glimpses of what Celia could be or what she once was.

One of the themes of the show is grief, but Nancy isn't the only one who is bereft. Celia grieves for the life she felt she deserved and never got—a fact that at once enrages and devastates her.

Celia's life has become a giant joke that she can't seem to get on track. And she knows deep down inside that she's the butt of the joke and it's incredibly painful for her. She believes that her daughter really is fat, and that she has the most horrible husband on the planet. Dean's actually not that bad, though she has to deal with the fact that *he's* been cheating on *her* because he's the mid-level asshole. She feels she has nowhere to go, so she's going to make his life a living hell. That's why Celia is such a bitch. If Celia really came to terms with who she was, she wouldn't be able to go on.

Celia's torture campaign extends to her two daughters, especially Isabel, who she regularly torments about her weight. What's it like to utter some of those vitriolic lines to a young girl?

You know, I had a conversation with Allie Grant about this at the beginning of this season, because they were furthering this story line with me calling her the fat kid. I started to worry about her as a young actress, so I pulled her aside and said, "You could be anorexic and Celia would still think you were fat, because this isn't about you. It's about Celia. I don't want you to start thinking that you're fat, because you're not." In Celia's eyes, she's fat, and that has to do with Celia's own feelings about her weight, beauty, aging, and her place in the community. It's the reason she got rid of Quinn: She was just too beautiful and too sexual. If Celia had the thin daughter around, she'd feel threatened. So, it's not about her daughters, per se, but about her own self-perception. She's a self-consciously unhappy brazen woman. And, sadly, she wholeheartedly believes she's doing the right thing.

You've had to tackle a lot of tough material—combative dialogue, physical encounters with Mary-Louise Parker, Romany Malco, and Kevin Nealon, and emotional story lines involving breast cancer, marital breakdowns, relationship meltdowns. What were the most challenging moments for you?

It was tough pretending I was crapping on that toilet in "Good Shit Lollipop," let me tell you [*laughs*]. The most difficult was the scene in the nightclub with Conrad in the first season, because I was scared of the "jungle fever" line. It was really hard for me to say because it was very racist, and it was really hard to make it work. I was in a nightclub full of black people, and a couple of people turned around and said, "What the hell did she just say?" I would never liken myself to the genius of Carroll O'Connor, but I can imagine that when he played Archie Bunker, he had to think, How do I walk in there and be the biggest bigot on the planet and still make people like me and tune in every week? It's a really fine line. I remember when I first saw that "jungle fever" line, I said to Jenji, "This is racist," and she said, "Yeah, but Celia doesn't know that it's racist." Celia makes racial slurs to pretty much everybody. Like when I ask Lupita after the car accident, "Who hit me? Is she one of your maid friends?" That's just so awful. Celia doesn't even hear Lupita's retort. She's just not aware. I think when Elizabeth is more aware than Celia, it becomes a struggle for me as a performer. And then I run up to Jenji and go, "*Aahhhhhhh!*" [*Laughs*]

Celia and Nancy are probably the two smartest—and certainly most cynical—women in Agrestic, which initially draws them together. But Celia is needy, and Nancy is reserved, and both are self-absorbed, which proves to be a recipe for disaster.

Celia and Nancy may appear so far apart from each other, but they're actually very similar in that they're both pretty dissatisfied with their lives but they just keep going forward, hoping that things will get better. They are both making huge mistakes that they're completely unaware of. And they both walk through life with blinders on. They're like sharks—they have to keep swimming. Celia's relationship with Nancy is so tenuous. Deep down inside, I think Celia wants Nancy's life. As Celia perceives it, Nancy doesn't have the obnoxious husband, and she's thin, beautiful, and she used to have an infinite amount of money. She seems to have been left well off. Nancy just doesn't appear to struggle with the things that Celia struggles with. So when the opportunity arises to bust Silas [in the second season finale], Celia is really excited because her own life is so flawed. That's why she wanted Nancy to be her friend for so long.

Which scenes do you think best evoke the spirit of Celia?

The fight between Celia and Nancy. That's hugely telling of Celia. She is at the point where she so yearns for the companionship of this woman that she resorts to a five-year-old's behavior. She makes it worse for herself in the long run. What Celia has been trying to do is to make it about Nancy, to open the door for Nancy to come in, and Nancy won't. And Celia desperately needs a friend. Pam's just an idiot—Becky Thyre is so great as Pam. I love her! I also like the scene where Celia comes into Nancy's kitchen with directions about what to do if you come into contact with a wildcat. She has a conversation about wanting to sleep with a woman because I think she's desperate to find any stimulation in her life. She'll try anything to go there. It sets up who Celia is: *I want an experience. I'm bored out of my mind.* I think it permeates throughout the entire show Celia's basic dissatisfaction. When she goes off on Dean about the "stupid atrium," that really exemplifies how bitter and angry she has become. The entire picture in that moment is going to be focused on that friggin' roof, in a "room where plants come to die," and she's the plant and she's dying. One of the other scenes that I love is when she puts on the

ELIZABETH PERKINS has been nominated for an Emmy, two Golden Globes, and two Satellite Awards for her role as Celia Hodes. Perkins made her feature-film debut in Ed Zwick's *About Last Night*. Her breakthrough performance was opposite Tom Hanks in *Big*, followed by an acclaimed performance in Barry Levinson's *Avalon*. Her other film credits include *The Doctor*; *He Said, She Said* with Kevin Bacon; *Indian Summer*; *The Flintstones* (as Wilma); *Miracle on 34th Street*; and *Moonlight and Valentino*. Other feature projects include *28 Days*, *Cats & Dogs*, and the animated *Finding Nemo* (as the voice of Coral). Her recent films include *Fierce People*, directed by Griffin Dunne, *The Ring Two*, *Must Love Dogs* opposite Diane Lane, and a starring role in the Showtime Independent film *Speak*.

Spliffing at the Seams: Celia Hodes
A Conversation with Costume Designer
amy STOFSKY

When we first meet Celia Hodes, she is the PTA president in a southern California upper-middle-class suburban school district, striving for a country club sexy look—and nearly pulling it off. But in the two seasons that we get to know her, we watch as her cancer diagnosis radically changes her aesthetic: Celia takes on a platinum blond flippy wig, and when she decides to run for Doug Wilson's seat on Agrestic's city council, she reinvents her look, transforming herself into a GOP Stepford Wife from hell. Costume Designer Amy Stofsky talks about the evolution of Celia Hodes's wardrobe.

Turning Elizabeth into Celia must have been quite a challenge.

In season one, Celia's look was very constructed. We did a lot of dresses. In season two, especially when she started running for the city council, it was changing her, too. Celia kept evolving, primarily because of the hair. So there were different stages to go through, because of the cancer, and also to accommodate that wig, which was over the top. We made a lot of 1940s clothes for Elizabeth. They didn't work as well as the fifties clothes. The wig was so suggestive of a reject Marilyn Monroe that it was easy to go into that and keep her in as many "Jordan almond" colors as we could allow for a fifties pilot. The biggest obstacle was Celia's house, because its decor was so tropical. We didn't want her to look like a part of the furniture.

You made a lot of her clothes?

Yes, we made a number of pieces for Celia because it was easier. Sometimes it's just easier because you can use fabrics that work better on an actor. The clothes aren't always in the stores when you need them, because you're usually one season off, so there's just not always enough to choose from because everything is too heavy for the climate out here. So if you want to put somebody in a suit, you don't want a nubby, heavy, wooly-bully suit—your actors will hate you, and it's too damn hot. So if you can't find the stuff, you just make it in a fabric, like a tropical wool, or something else they won't be totally miserable in.

What story lines let you run wild with Celia?

I loved when she gives everything away, because it gave me the opportunity to start over. And I loved "'Lude Awakening," because that Foxy Lady satin roller-skating jacket was so funny and ridiculous [*laughs*]. Elizabeth Perkins is brilliant!

Little Boxes on the Hillside: The Hodes House

A Conversation with Set Decorator

Julie Bolder

Set Decorator Julie Bolder helps us navigate the floral and fauna that enliven the paper-thin walls of Celia's "ridiculous" house.

It's easy to forget that Celia and Nancy's homes are built out of the same model when you walk through Celia's door. Their aesthetics couldn't be more different.

It's true. All of these people have the same items in their house, but it's how they're combined, their style, their personality. If they were all painted like they would have been when they were brand-new, you would think they were all the same. It's when you add the personality, the colors, the layering, that they become a story.

Which was harder to imagine when you first set out to decorate, Nancy's home or Celia's?

Celia's, because there were so many ways we could have taken her visually. It's really a challenge to go huge and bold and big and in-your-face, and still have it look decent. Her curtains in her bedroom are big wide stripes, then she has these big florals in her bedroom, and we had everything in there custom made because you can't just go buy that stuff. I've got twelve different patterns in her family room and kitchen. The trick is to have them all in the same room together.

You had an opportunity to redecorate when Celia gave away all of the furniture after the cargo plane crashed into their home in the first season.

Yes, although she ended up buying back her own furniture. A lot of the house was exactly the same: It just kind of went out and came back in.

The house reflects Celia's bossy nature. You can tell Isabel isn't allowed to decorate her own room, and certainly Dean wasn't allowed to weigh in on the house either.

It all screams Celia and that's the point. Celia is so controlling, it's going to be my way or no way. You know that Isabel had no input in her bedroom. And in the master bedroom, obviously Dean had no input there, because would he really be sleeping with giant tropical flowers behind his head on his pillows? [*Laughs*] Probably not.

THE DOPE on . . .

Celia Hodes's Kif and Kin: The Younger Daughter

ISABEL

HODES

She's been dubbed "Isabelly" by her mother, and "shit girl" by her middle school classmates, but Celia's precocious younger daughter will not be beaten down. Armed with a thick skin and an even sharper tongue, the savvy preteen fearlessly goes toe-to-toe with her mother, fending off her unending stream of insults, not to mention an arsenal of nutritionists, diets, "incentive outfits," surveillance cameras, and daily weigh-ins with cutting retorts and defensive eating. The sniping devolves into all-out war when Celia secretly replaces Isabel's secret stash of chocolates with Ex-Lax, causing her daughter to literally lose

her shit in art class (which is how she earned her horrible nickname). Celia claims her intentions are in earnest as she explains to an enraged Dean, "I was just hoping for some nice loose doodies. Clean the girl out a bit. . . . Excuse me for wanting my daughter to be thin and attractive so that the world may be her oyster. . . . It's cold and cruel out there for fat girls" ("Good Shit Lollipop"). Revenge will be Isabel's, who employs her own stomach-churning switcheroo: With her ego bolstered by her father's unconditional love and support, Isabel replaces Celia's TrimSpa diet pills with Imodium AD tablets, which constipates her mother for days.

The battle of the bulge gets sidelined by Celia's breast cancer diagnosis, which reveals a humane side of Isabel's mother hitherto unseen by the Hodes kids. Isabel may proceed with mistrust, caution, and terror, but death—or the promise of it—becomes Celia. The girl can't resist cozying up to this new-and-improved version of her mother, who lets her raid vending machines, drink regular soda, and eat cheeseburgers, and even joins in on the binge. And, for the first time ever, mother and daughter find a way to bond when they are visited by Gran Pat (played by Concetta Tomei)—Celia's rail thin, churchgoing, narcissistic, one-woman-Gestapo mother—who upbraids Isabel's "Jew hair" and penchant for junk food, and excoriates Celia for raising her daughter "like a Gypsy," "giving away furniture," and marrying Dean, "who isn't man enough to stop her" ("Higher Education"). Finally Isabel discovers the source of her mother's exacting expectations, and recognizes in her a kindred spirit, especially when she learns that as a girl, Celia would remove the springs from the scale to keep her own diet-obsessed mother from weighing her.

Alas, the bond is short-lived: As soon as Celia's cancer goes into remission, her bitch flag starts waving at full mast, beginning with her reprimand of Isabel and her playdate, Peggy Lee (see "Isabel Hodes's Special Bud: Peggy Lee"), whom she catches in a lip-lock during a game of "publicist and celebrity." Celia warns her, "You cannot become a les-

bian just because you don't want to lose weight. The only girl you should be seeing is Jenny Craig. I know, you see people like Rosie O'Donnell and you think, 'Hey, she can find love.' But that's not where lesbianism is going, Isabel. Look at *The L Word*!" Isabel does not let her mother have the last word. "I knew it wouldn't last. . . . You're feeling better, aren't you? You're not gonna die," she says. "'Cause when you think you're going to die, you're a much better person" ("The Godmother").

The final nail in the coffin of their relationship is pounded during Celia's city council campaign, when a scout approaches Isabel about modeling for Huskeroos, "a clothing line for larger children." Isabel is as ecstatic at the prospect of doing commercials as Celia is mortified—the company's mottos include "Huskeroos lets you be you" and "The bigger the better, the Huskeroos sweater." But Dean's recent firing from the law firm decides in favor of Little Miss Hodes. Once Isabel becomes the family's main breadwinner—and, as she tells her new accountant, Doug Wilson, in a hauntingly mini-Celia manner, she's making "big hunks of cheddar" ("Crush Girl Love Panic")— everyone in the family is beholden to her. She appoints her loyal, devoted father as the signatory of her trust and the manager of her new, lucrative modeling career, and cuts her mother out of the deal. When her parents discuss separating after Celia divulges the news of her affair with Doug, she bellows from her bedroom, "I wanna live with Dad!" ("Yeah. Like Tomatoes").

Father and daughter revel in their newfound freedom, watching cartoons together, eating big bowls of sugary cereal, and dripping milk on the couch. Isabel can't undo the careful conditioning of the previous regime, and immediately heads to the kitchen for paper towels, but Dean stops her and encourages her to leave the mess. "Mom's not here," he tells her. Isabel, however, is far more perceptive than her father. "She'll be back. . . . Mom is Voldemort. You may have reduced her to vapor for now, but she's out there, gathering her strength. Don't you know that?" ("Pittsburgh").

Isabel may have inherited her father's metabolism, according to her mother, but thankfully she also has his heart. In order to protect that heart, as well as her sharp mind, she has had to pick up a few traits from her mother for better and for worse: a brazen demeanor, a sardonic wit, and a watchfulness that borders on paranoia, which save her soul in the house of Hodes.

Isabel Hodes's Special Bud

Peggy Lee,
played by Olivia Sui

Peggy Lee is Isabel's friend who helps her invent a steamy game consisting of casting one girl as a fawning publicist, the other, her sexy celebrity client. Isabel always nabs the role of the starlet, throwing herself into a series of provocative poses, eliciting adulation from her Chinese friend, whose job is to gasp, "You are sooooo hot." Flattery gets Peggy a tender-lovin' make-out session with her playdate, which is abruptly brought to a halt when Celia catches them in the act and exhorts for using lesbianism as a way of getting out of losing weight. Isabel scoffs at the notion, declaring, "I love Peggy, and she loves me." Celia quips, "She's a little Asian girl. They look like boys already. You might as well go for the real deal." Though Peggy tries to defend her femininity—"I have boobs!"—Celia takes one look at her tiny chest, shuts her down, and sends her home. Peggy gets the last word when she calls her grandparents for a ride. Speaking in Chinese, she tells them, "[Mrs. Hodes] says I can't play with her daughter anymore because she doesn't like immigrants and she thinks we should move out of her neighborhood."

But Isabel is the one who gets the fuzzy end of the Splenda-sweetened lollipop. As she pedals her bike down the street, she spies her girlfriend mashing faces with a boy. Isabel is devastated to realize that what was an expression of passion for her was merely a practice session for Peggy. So she is confused when her friend tells her, "You look really hot." Still, she happily takes the compliment. "Yeah," says Peggy, "you're really sweaty."*

In addition to her appearance on *Weeds*, OLIVIA SUI has also guest starred on the USA Network series *Monk*.

*All quotes from "The Godmother"

HASHING IT OUT WITH...
allie grant

Is it true that *Weeds* was your first major acting job? Members of the cast and crew say your nickname on the set is "Money Grant" because you always nail your scenes on the first take.

[*Laughs*] It's true. I had just moved to L.A. from Tupelo, Mississippi, two weeks before I auditioned. I was scared to death. There were, like, ten people sitting in there and I was terrified and intimidated. I found out a few weeks later I got the part. I was just so excited to be on the same set as Elizabeth Perkins!

You are a very quick study with incredibly keen instincts, because you really bring Isabel to life.

Thank you. When I read the scenes between Celia and Isabel, or Dean and Isabel, I think, If I were really Isabel and this were real life, what would I do? How would I really perceive this in real life? I relate to Isabel, because she is very sassy, and so am I, and she stands up for what she believes in, and I try to put that into my performance, plus add a little bit of me in there because I want her to seem like a real, natural person. I really learn a lot from Elizabeth and Mary-Louise. Just watching them, the way they handle themselves and everything: I want to learn from them and take and try to mix it in with my own technique. I don't get to work a lot with Mary-Louise, but whenever I watch *Weeds* and I watch her, there's something about her eyes. She's not even speaking with her voice, just with her eyes, and it just makes it exquisite. It's the subtleties of her performance and Elizabeth's performance that make them so brilliant.

What did you think of Isabel Hodes when you first read the pilot script?

I didn't really know much about the role or the show because when my parents and I looked at the script, I was ten years old, and we'd only been out in L.A. for two weeks.

236

At first my parents were like, "I don't know, Allie." And then my mom was like, "No, this is gonna be a hit. Think about it: It's so fresh and it's new." I started thinking about it, and I was like, "Yeah, it's a really magnetic concept and it's so real." I mean, if you were widowed, you don't know for sure that you wouldn't be doing the same exact thing. I have to admit, I was eager to take any role at that point, but I am so glad I took this one because it is such an amazing thing to work on. I've learned so much on the show from Elizabeth Perkins and Mary-Louise Parker, just being in their presence and watching how they work. It's really incredible.

Do you like Isabel?

Oh my God, yes. Isabel is such an amazing character to play. I love that Isabel is the only sane person in her family. And the whole look thing: There are so many girls out there that are beautiful but they don't wear a size zero. It's inspiring to other girls my age who look that way—it's normal to look that way. Everyone wants to change something about themselves, but Isabel is comfortable in her own skin. She doesn't care what people think. She is just her own person, very independent. I think she is a great role model—she is sort of *my* role model.

Celia is constantly scrutinizing Isabel's appearance, and as a result Elizabeth has to throw some incredibly harsh words your way on a regular basis. Is that hard to take?

It's funny, whenever Elizabeth and I see each other during rehearsals, she comes up to me and hugs me and says, "I'm so sorry. You know I don't mean any of this. People think that I am the worst mother because I have to say these things to you." And I say, "Elizabeth, it's just the character. If I ever talked to my mother this way, I would be grounded forever!" I don't take it personally and neither does she when I say mean things back to her [as Isabel]. I was talking to Jenji, who said, "I just want to make sure that I'm not giving you a complex. I don't want you to think that you're fat." I was like, "No, I don't. I know it's just the role that I play." And I'm having fun because I get to say things back to Celia.

Isabel was able to get a rare glimpse into her mother's psyche when Celia suffers the double whammy of being diagnosed with breast cancer and being visited by her toxic mother, Gran Pat. Isabel discovers the source and depths of her mother's insecurities as she watches her maternal grandmother let loose her anti-Semitic, diet-obsessed, crazy church-lady wrath on the entire Hodes family. These insights seem to empower Isabel.

Yeah, I think for the first time, Isabel is like, Wow, my mom is actually a real person. I shouldn't go around ignoring her because she's a person with feelings and a personality, and her mom is doing to her the same thing that she's doing to me. Isabel finally began to understand her.

Do you think Isabel draws emotional strength from her father's unconditional love?

Yeah. Dean is a really great father and a perfect foil for Celia. And I think at the end of the day, he wants what Nancy Botwin wants, which is to live a normal life, and for everything to come together and work out. Isabel sees that and that's why she's so drawn to him and is so close to him. I always tell Andy [Milder], "I do not know what Isabel would do without you!" Next season Isabel just might be smoking weed because she has no one! So it's so good that Dean is there, because it would be awful if she didn't have anything. I love Andy. He is so sweet.

What have been some of your favorite scenes to do?

In the second season, I really loved "A.K.A. The Plant," when the Huskeroos lady recruited Isabel on the sidewalk [while Celia was campaigning for city council]. That was so much fun, because in rehearsals Elizabeth and I had to argue. It was all improv and I loved doing that. I loved "Crush Girl Love Panic" because Paul Mitchell was there and he was like, "Oh, honey, I'm gonna hook you up with some curly hair products. It's all for free, don't worry about it." He was really sweet. And I loved doing the season finale. We had a scene, just Andy and I, where we were on the couch watching cartoons, and while we were sitting there, we were just talking about life. Andy is just so down to earth.

Do your parents let you watch *Weeds*?

My parents will read a script and they'll say, "Okay, episode three seems fine for you to see, but episode five I'm not so sure about. That's a little racy." I'm always able to watch my scenes. But it depends on the episodes. The majority of the time I do get to watch the whole thing because I was there when it was made—it's not a big deal.

Weeds starts shooting in the spring, when school is still in session. Is it hard to get your homework done when you're working on the set?

My school is really relaxed and flexible, and I get to bring my work on the set. I'm able to do my homework with the studio teacher and, as long as I turn it in and it's correct, it doesn't matter how it gets done. My teachers are all pretty cool about that. And there are other actors in my class, like Charlie Stewart [*The Suite Life of Zack and Cody*, *Life with Bonnie*]. We're all pretty much connected to the business, which is pretty cool.

What's the set like when you're not in a scene or doing homework?

Well, for one thing, we have the coolest crew. We even have nicknames for some of the guys, like Pocket, who is one of our electrical guys—he has pockets everywhere to keep all the stuff in. There is another guy called Crash, because he rammed this huge big pole during the first episode of shooting, and it made this really loud noise. It's all fun and games around the set, and when the director yells cut, we're all goofing off, but when it's time to work we all buckle down and do our jobs. This past season, Hunter had a treasure hunt around the set for Alexander's birthday—those two are very close. Hunter had a balloon tied everywhere around the set, and Alexander would pop each one, because inside the balloon would be a clue to where the next balloon was. It was so cool.

ALLIE GRANT arrived in Los Angeles from Tupelo, Mississippi, in 2004 to pursue acting and, within weeks, landed *Weeds*, her first job. She regularly guest stars on the television series *The Suite Life of Zack and Cody* as Agnes, and will appear in the feature film *Fanboys*, directed by Kyle Newman.

Celia Hodes's Kif and Kin:
The Older Daughter

Quinn Hodes,
played by Haley Hudson

Quinn Hodes is everything Celia finds most threatening in a teenage daughter: She's smart, surly, beautiful, and, worst of all, sexually active. So her mother feels justified in taking a guerilla approach to parenting by reading her diary and trying to recruit Nancy Botwin—the mother of Quinn's boyfriend, Silas—to hide a nanny-cam in Silas's room to capture him and her daughter having sex. Quinn recognizes the nanny-cam, which is cloaked in a pink teddy bear, from the time Celia placed it in the pantry to catch Isabel sneaking food. She intercepts it and decides to beat her mother at her own game by turning the lens on her father and his favorite tennis instructor. Celia pops in the surveillance tape, expecting to see her daughter and Silas going at it, only to be mortified by the sight of Dean screwing Helen Chin (played by Michelle Krusiec), who is sliding a tennis racket up his ass. Quinn drives a stake through Celia's heart by cutting to herself in her room in the final frames of the video, waving, mouthing the words "Fuck you," and flipping her the bird. Quinn suffers the consequence of being sent off to a Mexican boarding school, but she hardly seems to care: She spends her final days in Agrestic coloring her hair, loading two thousand songs onto her iPod, and telling neither her little sister nor her boyfriend that she is leaving with no plans to return. Isabel is baffled. And Silas feels abandoned and downright heartbroken. "Not a sentimentalist," says Celia. "All Quinn cares about is Quinn. She takes after her father that way" ("Free Goat").

HALEY HUDSON appeared in the film Freaky Friday, and has guest starred in the series Lizzie McGuire.

THE DOPE on ...

Dean

According to his wife, Celia, Dean Hodes is "a fucking loser with a body shaped like a Cadbury Easter egg only with hair all over it. But on the plus side, he's tidy and he's got a decent job, so maybe it evens out" ("A.K.A. The Plant"). To his Agrestic neighbors, he appears to be a modest, nebbishy lawyer (who "can get myself off," as he boasts to Nancy Botwin and Doug Wilson ("Dead in the Nethers")); the hapless Jewish husband to the quintessential shiksa wife; and the devoted father to two daughters, one naughty, one nice. But our first introduction—which comes through the proverbial back door—gives another,

HODES

perhaps misleading impression of him as an ass when tales of a raunchy assignation involving tennis instructor Helen Chin (played by Michelle Krusiec), a lubed-up racquet, and his *tuchus* make the gossip circuit. Lest the veracity of the rumor be in question, his older daughter, Quinn (see "Celia Hodes's Kif and Kin: The Older Daughter: Quinn Hodes"), captures the action with Celia's nanny-cam meant to surveil the adolescent sexploits of her and her boyfriend, Silas Botwin, which ensures that the sordid footage ends up in her mother's hands. Dean is as described, and a lot more.

Celia serves Dean a preliminary helping of revenge for his affair, with two Ambien and the graze of an electric razor against his sleeping head. The vitriol Celia spews when she faces off his mistress over martinis at the local strip mall bar make Dean's transgression seem rational—an act of self-preservation. As Celia alternates between eviscerating and bonding with Helen, she confesses, "He's not what I thought he'd be. Rich. Powerful. Faithful. He just turned out to be another mid-level asshole. And that makes me Mrs. Mid-level Asshole" ("Free Goat"). But Dean is also a mensch and a fierce protector of his family. He cares for Celia when she is undergoing treatment for breast cancer, even though she's given away all of her clothes and half of their furniture out of spite after a cargo plane crashes into their house. He gallantly rids their home of a toxin even more malignant than Celia's tumor: her mother, Pat (played by Concetta Tomei). And he always remembers their wedding anniversary, kindly and generously, no matter how rough things get between them.

Still, Celia is determined to even the score with an infidelity of her own, and her cancer diagnosis only ratchets up the urgency. She scores with Nancy's "carpenter" (and Dean's future clandestine business partner), Conrad Shepard, and dares to report the news to Dean. With mission "Shock and Awe" dutifully accomplished, they enter a full-blown, day-long war. Though the combat of the couple's feverish truth session yields nearly two decades' worth of grievances, resentments, and misunderstandings, it reconnects Dean and Celia for the first time in years, and temporarily salvages their deeply troubled marriage.

Dean may compromise his own needs for the sake of his relationship and falter when Celia decides to ship Quinn to a Mexican boarding school, but he fights to the death for his younger daughter, Isabel. He tries to soothe his little girl after she is overcome by an explosive bout of diarrhea at school, destroying her pants, and far worse, her reputation. "One day you'll think back on it and, well, it will still feel painfully embarrassing, but it will make for a terrific story," he tells her, attempting to find the silver lining of her shit-stained underwear. "I had to throw my pants into the woods," a mortified Isabel explains. "And *that's* part of the story," Dean offers. He quickly learns that Celia is the culprit—and an unapologetic one at that. Dean reams her: "I should call child protective services and have you arrested! . . . I hope our children survive you!" So when Celia announces during their nightly ablution rituals that she "hasn't shit for three days," he can't resist gloating over her colonic misfortune. "Could it be? Newton's third law of motion—or lack of motion, in your case—illustrated right here in our bathroom: For every action there is an equal and opposite reaction" ("Good Shit Lollipop").

New marital troubles brew when Celia runs for Doug's seat in the city council, passing over Dean as her campaign manager in favor of her sweet but dumb friend Pam Gruber.

So Dean is only too happy to fend off his wife as she tries to sabotage Isabel's Huskeroos audition and first commercial shoot. He proudly stands by his daughter's side as Paul Mitchell himself styles her hair, encouraging her to revel in her beauty, and he shares in the delight as the director and stylists boot the menacing Celia from the set. But while Dean's love for Isabel is genuine, his motivation to help her with her burgeoning modeling career isn't entirely altruistic. He becomes dependent on his daughter's income when, instead of making partner, he is unceremoniously fired and launches into a Tourettic tirade in the lobby of his office building that gets him Tasered in front of the entire corporate law firm. He is earning money on the down low as Nancy's legal counsel for her illegal business, but it isn't enough to cover Quinn's boarding school, Celia's city council campaign, and the high cost of living in Agrestic. And while Isabel has his back on the home front after losing his job, Dean feels like his stock is plummeting everywhere else.

Weed, and all that comes with it, has for Dean always served as a reliable escape from his misery. But Celia—the one person in Agrestic who isn't apprised of Nancy's business—is indirectly creeping into his safe haven. He suspects that his grow house

colleague is the very same man who slept with his wife. Dean asks his pals, "Is Conrad a popular name in the African-American community?" ("Cooking with Jesus"). Dean confronts Conrad, who fesses up and offers the cuckolded husband a free punch. But Dean, who has never engaged in a fistfight, is caught off guard and pitifully asks for a rain check. "Dude, you're taking pussy to a whole new level," marvels Conrad ("Last Tango in Agrestic"). When Dean finally cashes in and throws his punch—at the front door of the grow house—he runs for his life, even though Conrad isn't chasing him.

Dean faces bigger, more lasting problems when he buoyantly signs on to become City Councilman Doug's campaign manager. In the midst of his firing, he accidentally leaves the election paperwork at his office, and as a result fails to get Doug's name on the ballot. It's an inadvertent betrayal greater than Dean could have ever imagined: He has essentially handed over a victory to Doug's mortal enemy, Celia, and robbed his best friend of the very thing that identifies him. Doug returns the favor in kind by having a surprisingly hot-and-heavy love affair with Celia. What's worse, she falls madly in love with Doug, and tells an

incredulous Dean that she's leaving him. He says, "But Doug hates you. . . . Unbelievable." She replies, "Why? You are *so* the kind of guy this stuff happens to" ("Yeah. Like Tomatoes").

Celia tries to crawl back into their home and Dean's good graces, but he has finally, in his wife's words, "grown a sack" and kicks her out. While Dean appears to suffer from an ongoing internal battle between being a man or a mouse, shrewd and insightful Isabel—who is slowly if reluctantly turning into a mini-Celia (albeit one with a capacity to sympathize with others)—may be able to keep Dean strolling down the right path.

HASHING IT OUT WITH . . .
andy milder

What did you think of Dean Hodes when you first read him on the page?

To be honest, Dean didn't seem like much in the pilot script because we didn't know where he was going, so I didn't know if he was right for me. I know that sounds dumb because you'd think, I could make anything out of it. But I just wasn't sure what to make of him. But I quickly fell in love with the guy.

Rumor has it that you had to shave your head for the role.

Getting my head shaved was a real bummer [*laughs*]. I was not pleased about that. I had a very cursory audition for the pilot. Showtime hadn't realized the show was going to be so big, and that Dean was going to play a rather huge role. When they realized how big it was going to be, they said, "We need to have a much larger actor." To make a very long story a lot shorter, it came down to me and two other guys. I got a phone call the night after the audition [for the series] saying that Dean was soon going to have his head shaved, and, while the other guys were okay with it, the part would be mine if I was willing to shave my head. I couldn't turn it down, because at that point I already knew Dean, and I loved him.

Dean is an endearing nebbish, whose greatest achievement, I think, is being a great father.

Yeah, he really loves Isabel. In my opinion, being a good dad is his most appealing quality and his only solace in his life, especially right now. He's such a lovable loser. When Celia announces she's leaving Dean for Doug, she is absolutely right when she she asks why he's surprised. That is who he is. Don't get me wrong: I'm not talking about Dean's relationship with Celia. I'm talking about a Dean as a character in the world of Dean.

248

How did Dean find his way into your heart?

Well, he's kind of irrepressible. And he's fairly smart—smart enough to be a lawyer, though I certainly wouldn't call him the smartest guy on the block. He married Celia, after all, though she certainly isn't the same person I imagine he fell in love with. I like that he's a family man, and cares about his daughters: He obviously keeps in touch with Quinn. And I love that he's pals with Doug and Nancy. Actually, when I first started playing Dean, my original thought was that he had a crush on Nancy. There is some complexity to him, which keeps it interesting. Remember, when we first meet him, he's screwing a tennis instructor who shoves a tennis racquet up his ass. Dean is willing to do some crazy shit. I really dug the fact that he secretly gets into business with Nancy. He doesn't talk much about it; he just does it. And when he gets paid, he realizes, no IRS and no Celia. It's kind of his way of saying, "Screw Celia. I'm out." He's escaping without escaping.

What do you think of Dean's decision to go into business with Nancy?

This is one thing I have not yet reconciled: Why isn't Dean making more in the dope business, and relying so much on his daughter's modeling career to pay his bills? Certainly he's making some nice side money with Nancy. But seriously, it made perfect sense to me for Dean to get into business with Nancy in the same way that it made perfect sense that Doug should be in the business. Here's Dean, who buys every baked good that Nancy made: "Fuck it, I'll take the whole basket," he says. The guy desperately needs escape. He's screwing a tennis instructor. He's getting a racquet shoved up his ass. He's smoking a lot of weed. He's buying a motorcycle. He loves his wife, but his family life is very difficult. So for him to have another form of escape, to be able to go somewhere and watch a plant grow, is a treat for him, whether or not he wants to admit it.

What are some of your favorite scenes so far?

My absolute favorite is when Dean gets Tasered in the lobby of his law firm. What a joy that the writers did that for me. It was so funny. I also really love the scene when Dean is sitting in the Mexican restaurant with Doug, Sanjay, and Alejandro, and starts to figure out who Conrad is. I remember getting the script in my room and seeing the line, "Conrad. Is that a popular name in the African-American community?" Oh Jesus, that's so goddamn funny. You can see where it's going. What I like about Dean is, I don't think he planned to throw that punch at Conrad. I think that Dean wanted to plan it, had every intention of planning it, but did not plan it because he was afraid to plan it. And that's why I love when you see him in the moment of rage, he opens the door, and *BAM!* And then he realizes what he's done and runs the fuck away. There's a scene that at first I didn't want to accept praise for, but now I will, in which Dean is polishing his new motorcycle and he looks up at Celia and tells her he's managing Isabel's career. I think it is a defining moment for Dean. He's a man pent up, and here he is exploding.

As Dean, you have your work cut out for you, fending off a perpetually disappointed and frequently enraged Celia, managing Isabel's burgeoning career as a Huskeroos model, and keeping illicit business affairs on the down low. What is the hardest part about playing Dean?

251

Honestly? Trying to keep up with the brilliant acting around me. I'm not saying that I'm not able to. But I'm constantly awestruck. Elizabeth is phenomenal—I adore her, and God she's fun to work with! And Mary-Louise may be the best actress on television. Justin Kirk is brilliant. And so is Kevin—I think this is his best work, and I've always thought he was funny. I feel like I'm a salmon constantly swimming upstream and I want to keep up with salmon around me.

Are there other characters on the show that you relate to?

I love Doug—he kills me. And I love Conrad, and Celia. Celia's friend Pam is another great one. I think Becky Thyre is hysterical. I love her character and I love her. I really love all of them. And I love how the writers write with a long-range view of where they want these characters to go. They don't write just to write. It's shocking how smart they are. Like that hair-pulling scene between Celia and Nancy: "BE MY FRIEND!" It's so wonderful—one of my absolute favorite scenes in the series. Here's this moment where Celia pulls Nancy's hair—okay, fine. But it develops Celia's character.

Do you ever offer your feedback to the writers, or make suggestions about what you'd like to see Dean do?

I try not to give much feedback on the show because I really like what I'm given. The material is so smart and so good that it's kind of hard for me to say anything. Each time I got a new script, I felt like I was getting another chapter of *The Da Vinci Code* because I felt like I was left hanging every week and couldn't wait to read the next one. I'm very lucky because I'm a fan of the show as well as being on it. In general the writers have been very open to listening to ideas that I might have. The directors and the writers are willing to go the extra mile on the show. Everyone wants to listen: the actors, the writers, the directors. It's very open and very inviting, creatively.

Can you share something about yourself that might surprise viewers?

Sure. It was my choice in life either to be a lawyer or to be an actor. I stood in front of a post office with my LSAT scores in hand, ready to apply to law school, debating between trying again, because I knew I could do better, or throwing them in the trash and heading to L.A. to pursue acting. Needless to say, after sitting in front of the post office for three hours, I threw them in the trash. And now I play a lawyer on TV.

Despite being accepted to Northwestern University, ANDY MILDER went to UC Berkeley to study economics and get away from acting—and failed in his quest, though he did graduate with honors. Moving to Los Angeles, Andy was quite fortunate in finding acting work, appearing in *Apollo 13*, *The West Wing*, *Six Feet Under*, *CSI: NY* (with an Israeli accent), *House*, *Boston Legal*, *Dharma & Greg*, *Tracey Takes On* (written in part by Jenji Kohan), *Star Trek: Deep Space Nine* and *Voyager*, *Armageddon*, *Transformers*, and most recently, *Ugly Betty*. Andy currently coruns the single most successful fake acting class in Los Angeles, Definition: Actor (definitionactor.com).

THE DOPE on . . .

Pam

Celia Hodes's Fronds Indeed:
The Best Friend by Default

GruBer

Celia may verbally abuse her and threaten to ditch her for Nancy at any given moment, but she can always count on Pam Gruber to be her fiercest and most faithful ally. Still, Celia worries that by publicly accepting Pam as a friend, she will be perceived as the queen of the dipshits. Pam doesn't seem to care, though. Insistently optimistic and weirdly lovable, she is determined to find the silver lining in the most threadbare of clouds, and will do anything to be included with the other mothers. She'll happily take on the bake sale in the PTA; flee a meeting in pursuit of Celia and the last quaalude on earth; or take a stripper fitness class, even though her lack of upper body strength makes using the pole difficult for her and she is ultimately forced to quit the class when her husband tells her he's worried she'll "go lesbo on him, like when [she] took folk guitar" ("Corn Snake").

Pam finds her greatest opportunity to shine for Celia when her friend announces her plans to challenge Doug Wilson for his seat on the city council. Eager to step up to the plate, Pam provides all the advice and legwork of a campaign manager in hopes that Celia will anoint her; Celia does so begrudgingly, since her own husband, Dean, has decided to work for Doug. Maybe Celia isn't entirely wrong when she dismisses Pam's ideas as "retarded"—Pam suggests slogans like "Making Friends" after Doug blows up at Celia for running against him, or "Celia Hodes: It's Time for Change," paired with the image of "a big clock, and, like, instead of numbers, we have nickels and dimes and quarters. Get it? *Time* for *change*? Isn't that cute?" ("Corn Snake").

But Pam is nothing if not resilient, and she's also thorough: While working the campaign phone bank, she doesn't flinch when she dials the number for "Mr. Fukhusen," Doug's vindictive nom de guerre. And her blissfully ignorant disposition doesn't allow her to comprehend what transpires in the Hodes' hallway when Celia pulls Nancy's hair and demands her friendship. Always one to look at the bright side, Pam declares, "You two are just like sisters" ("Nancy Botwin's Neighborhood"). She even agrees to put on the cumbersome, heavy Sober the Sasquatch costume and accompany Celia as she gives an antidrug lecture to the middle school, which quickly devolves into a humiliating riot led by Shane Botwin. Whether or not Celia wants her to bear witness to these moments, Pam is determined to stand by her side to cheer her victory against Doug, find the good in any bad situation, and be the go-to girl in a pinch.

Pam Gruber may be a dolt, but she has stuck by Celia's side, enduring a considerable amount of verbal abuse. What do you think of Pam?

I like Pam, and I love whenever I get the scripts and find out what I'm doing. I think the Sober the Sasquatch scene is one of the funniest, especially when Shane says to Celia, "I've seen you drunk at my house." I've played other characters that are kind of like Pam, who are happy in the way they are. When Celia is mean to Pam, I kind of don't mind it as Pam. It doesn't hurt Pam's feelings. I [as Pam] am enjoying the place where I am. In my own life, I've had a lot of friends that are kind of mean like Celia, and I just liked them anyway. I find them fun to be around because they're more exciting than people who are nice, in some ways [*laughs*].

Given the chance, Celia would drop Pam for Nancy in a heartbeat. Do you think she knows that?

Yeah. I feel like, as Pam, I know that Nancy is cooler and that Celia would rather be friends with her. I realize I'm not cool, but I'll follow her.

You and Elizabeth Perkins have great comic chemistry. What's it like working with her?

Elizabeth is great. She's really very friendly and very easy to talk to, and she's a great actress—very giving. When I do small parts, I try to make sure I don't step on anybody's toes or do anything that makes a lead actress mad [*laughs*]. But she's not like that. If I did something funny, she would be glad about it. And I've worked with actors who, when you're the supporting person, you better not be too funny or they'll get mad at you. I love her.

What kind of feedback have you gotten from *Weeds* viewers?

I actually looked on the message board one time to see if they were talking about her, and it made me so happy. There's one thread after the episode where Celia wins for city council seat, and there's a thread called "Pam is the Best Friend Ever." [*Laughs*] There was this little thread, and one person wrote, "I just love Pam. I can just imagine her, sitting at her little computer, sending out her e-mails with dancing kittens on them." Another said, "I was so excited to see how excited Pam was that Celia won than for Celia winning. Yay for Pam! Boo for Celia! She wants to take our weed away!" [*Laughs*] I think all the people on the message boards are mostly stoners and they all discuss, "I can't believe Celia wants to take our weed away." "Finally Nancy's smoking."

What do you do when you're not being Pam?

I'm married to a syndicated cartoonist, known as Tony Millionaire [Scott Richardson], and we're working on a show for Cartoon Network called *The Drinky Crow Show*—I did some voices for that. I'm also in this all-women group called the Write Club, and we each write and perform ten-minute autobiographical pieces every month.

A prolific comedic actress, BECKY THYRE has guest starred on *Six Feet Under*, *Curb Your Enthusiasm*, *Arrested Development*, *Just Shoot Me!*, *My Wife and Kids*, and *Mr. Show with Bob and David*, among others, and provided the voices for the cartoons *God Hates Cartoons* and *The Oblongs*.

Celia Hodes's Fronds Indeed:
The Hypo-Christian Bitch Moms

Maggie Reynolds,
played by Tressa DiFiglia

No sooner does Celia Hodes get diagnosed with breast cancer than one of her minions, the Eve Harrington–esque "Hypo-Christian Bitch Mom" Maggie Reynolds, wrests the PTA presidency away from her and assumes the position for herself because "we need a reliable and healthy leader" ("The Punishment Lighter"). Two-faced Maggie, who revels in prurient, schadenfreude-charged gossip, especially where Celia is concerned, rationalizes that the deposed president isn't "programmed to feel" ("Free Goat"). But in Maggie's skewed moral world, jokes about Jesus Christ are too profane to tolerate—ever. So what if Agrestic Elementary is a public school? It doesn't stop Maggie from calling an emergency PTA meeting when she catches wind that Shane Botwin and his uncle Andy are selling "Chris Died for Your Sins" T-shirts on the school grounds (and is all too eager to start the meeting without Celia, who is still officially president at the time). Justice will ultimately be served in Celia's favor: She not only recovers her health, but her power, too, when she discovers with great pleasure that the community is being redistricted, sending self-righteous Maggie to another school, and better still, out of Agrestic.

Alison Alderson,
played by Shawn Schepps

Alison Alderson has aspirations only to be a devoted follower once she sets her sights on the right leader. An erstwhile apostle of Celia's, she switches allegiances to Maggie when she senses that the power structure within the PTA is shifting. On the one hand, Maggie shares her Christian values, and isn't shy about imposing them on the school board and the student body. But there's another part of Alison that never stops liking Celia, who saunters into a PTA meeting soon after her breast cancer diagnosis, wearing a pink satin roller-skating jacket with the words "Foxy Lady" emblazoned on the back, puffing on a cigarette, and blissed out on quaaludes. The sight of her reminds Alison of her own fun young years, when she had her own satiny jacket. Hers read "Big Stuff" . . . sigh. That was then. Now Alison has bigger issues on her plate, like Shane Botwin's sale of "Chris Died for Your Sins" T-shirts ("We don't joke about the Lord, Jesus Christ," she tells Nancy Botwin) and finding out who killed her beloved pet cat, Chester ("Fashion of the Christ").

HASHING IT OUT WITH . . .
SHAWN SCHEPPS

You are the only person who serves on the writing staff and on the cast of *Weeds*, playing the role of Alison Alderson, a PTA mother. How did you swing that?

I was a kid actor—I was in an episode of *The Brady Bunch*, which I never used to tell anyone. I started writing in my twenties and left acting behind. I got a call from Jenji's office asking me if I still had my SAG card, and the next thing I knew, I was one of the PTA moms.

The PTA moms could have blended together as a Greek chorus, but they quickly distinguish themselves: Maggie is ambitious, power hungry, and eager to wrest control from Celia, and Pam is a kindhearted dolt. What aspects of Alison's character did you most want to bring out?

I wanted to make her the more insecure and more neutral of the PTA moms. We see that really come to light in "'Lude Awakening," when Celia comes into the PTA meeting wearing her Foxy Lady satin jacket. I had Alison relishing memories of her youth as the fat girl in the jacket.

Celia Hodes is like a blowtorch in those PTA meetings. Is it daunting to play opposite Elizabeth?

No. We hang and talk and sometimes we'll smoke cigarettes together. But when I was acting with her as Celia, my character, Alison, went immediately into intimidation mode, which is how I became her follower. Writing Celia and hanging with Elizabeth—I totally get it. As a person Elizabeth is nothing like Celia, and you'd think I'd think that in my mind, that I would go to who Elizabeth is, and who this character is. But that's not how it happens when you step on that stage. You go right into who *your* character is, and who she happens to be playing against, and you both enter a whole other realm. When I'm in a scene with her, as Alison I feel two inches tall. It's odd, because the minute they yell cut, we return to being Shawn and Elizabeth, and there's camaraderie and joking and secrets and stuff about our lives. That's all a testament to Elizabeth and her amazing talent. She turns on Celia and you don't remember she's Elizabeth Perkins.

Do you like performing alongside the actors for whom you write?

Yeah. As writers and producer, we don't get a lot of time to hang with the actors, but when you're sitting waiting for shots and setups and scenes, you do. When I went down onto the set, I was an actor, and when I went upstairs to the writers' room, I was a writer, even when I was in actor clothes and actor makeup. My relationships changed so much when I was working with the actors. It's fun being in the scenes with them, and being able to hang out. I love cracking them up. I had this one scene with Mary-Louise, where I told her not to joke about our Lord Jesus Christ, and she couldn't stop laughing. We'd have to cut, and this went on and on. We had an actor moment together where we were cracking each other up. I probably would have never had that with her. The cast are all really good, awesome people.

A Los Angeles native and erstwhile child actor of stage and screen, SHAWN SCHEPPS guest starred in an episode of *The Brady Bunch*. As an adult, she's appeared in *The Terminator*, *Betrayed*, *Racing with the Moon*, and most recently as Alison Alderson, the PTA mom, on the first season of *Weeds*. An accomplished playwright, she has written the plays *The Steven Weed Show*; *Conspicuous Consumption*; *Mary Had a Little Cult*; *Group*, which she also directed; and the one-woman show *End of the Night*. Her screenplays include *Encino Man*, *Son in Law*, *Drumline*, and the independent feature *Lip Service*, which she also directed. She has also written and directed *L.A. Woman* for Disney's Sunday Night at the Movies.

appendixes

weeds episode guide
Titles and Credits

SEASON ONE:

1001: "You Can't Miss the Bear," written by Jenji Kohan, directed by Brian Dannelly

1002: "Free Goat," written by Jenji Kohan, directed by Brian Dannelly

1003: "Good Shit Lollipop," written by Roberto Benabib, directed by Craig Zisk

1004: "Fashion of the Christ," written by Jenji Kohan, directed by Burr Steers

1005: "Lude Awakening," written by Devon Shepard, directed by Lee Rose

1006: "Dead in the Nethers," written by Michael Platt and Barry Safchik, directed by Arlene Sanford

1007: "Higher Education," written by Shawn Schepps, directed by Tucker Gates

1008: "The Punishment Light," written by Rolin Jones, directed by Robert Berlinger

1009: "The Punishment Lighter," written by Matthew Salsberg, directed by Paul Feig

1010: "The Godmother," written by Jenji Kohan, directed by Lev L. Spiro

SEASON TWO:

2001: "Corn Snake," written by Jenji Kohan, directed by Craig Zisk

2002: "Cooking with Jesus," written by Jenji Kohan, directed by Craig Zisk

2003: "Last Tango in Agrestic," written by Roberto Benabib, directed by Bryan Gordon

2004: "A.K.A. The Plant," written by Matthew Salsberg, directed by Lev L. Spiro

2005: "Mrs. Botwin's Neighborhood," written by Rolin Jones, directed by Craig Zisk

2006: "Crush Girl Love Panic," written by Devon Shepard, directed by Tucker Gates

2007: "Must Find Toes," written by Michael Platt and Barry Safchik, directed by Chris Long

2008: "MILF Money," written by Shawn Schepps, directed by Craig Zisk

2009: "Bash," written by Rinne Groff, directed by Chris Misiano

2010: "Mile Deep and a Foot Wide," written by Rolin Jones, directed by Craig Zisk

2011: "Yeah. Like Tomatoes," written by Roberto Benabib and Matthew Salsberg, directed by Craig Zisk

2012: "Pittsburgh," written by Jenji Kohan, directed by Craig Zisk

BON(G) MOTS
The Lexicon of *Weeds*

A BOAT: in dominoes, when all the ends add up to twenty points

ALL BUN: no more hot dog (dickless)

BAKLAVA: an Armenian drug lord's special way of saying good-bye to new neighbors; also a sweet flaky dessert comprised of phyllo dough, walnuts or pistachios, and honey

BONES: dominoes

CANNABIS CLUB: according to Nancy and Heylia, the "Whole Foods of pot"; a place that provides marijuana for medicinal purposes. There are about one hundred cannabis clubs in the State of California operating since the passage of Proposition 215

FAKERY: Nancy and Andy's nickname for her cover business, a bakery named Breadsticks & Scones

GROW HOUSE: a house set up to grow hydroponic marijuana

HOOPTIE: a pimped-out old bucket of a car, like Conrad's '85 Cutlass Supreme

HYDROPONIC: a method of growing plants without soil

METH ADDICT: an expedient contractor who pays particular attention to detail; also a user of crystal meth

PROPOSITION 215: California's "medical marijuana" act, which passed in 1996. Allows people to possess and cultivate marijuana for personal medical use, with the referral of an authorized physician

RUACH: a Hebrew word for elan, spirit

SHAKE: the crummy weed remnants that end up at the bottom of the bag—seeds, twigs, leaf bits

SHWAG: low-grade, cheap pot; usually filled with seeds (which need to be removed before lighting up), and low in THC (requiring lots of smoking for little payoff)

THREE SWITCHIN' BITCHES: in dominoes, fifteen points

TRICHOMES: the crystals on marijuana buds, which possess the most concentrated form of THC

THe *weeds* PLAYLIST
Episode by Episode

SEASON ONE:

Theme Song: "Little Boxes,"
Malvina Reynolds

You Can't Miss the Bear

"Tuk Tuk," The Black Seeds
"David," Nellie McKay
"Singing in My Soul," Fly My Pretties
"Don't Stop the Music," Kava Kava
"With Arms Outstretched," Rilo Kiley
"A Doodlin' Song," Peggy Lee

Free Goat

"Don't Bite the Dick," David Allen Coe
"All the Trees of the Field Will Clap Their
    Hands," Sufjan Stevens

Good Shit Lollipop

"Ganga Baby," Michael Franti
"Snakes of Hawaii," Army Navy
"More than a Friend," All Too Much
"I Can't Move," Martin Creed
"Babalawo," Pasta Boys featuring Wunmi

Fashion of the Christ

"When We Were Young," Calahan
"Blood," Sons and Daughters
"Coffee's Cold," Abigail Washburn

'Lude Awakening

"The Laws Have Changed,"
    The New Pornographers

"If I Ever Leave This World Alive," Flogging Molly
"Wacky Tobacky," NRBQ

Dead in the Nethers

"Littlest Bird," The Be Good Tanyas
"Who Knows," Marion Black
"Now or Never," Jack Drag
"Ballerina," Leona Naess
"Air," Ephemera

Higher Education

"Work Song," Dan Reeder
"Step Away from the Cliff," Blue-Eyed Son
"It's Going," John Gold

The Punishment Light

"Cotton," The Mountain Goats
"Cariño Mio," Casolando

The Punishment Lighter

"I Will Be," Moses
"Bleed," The Negro Problem
"I Can Hurt People," Noam Weinstein

The Godmother

"Satan Lend Me a Dollar," Hill of Beans

SEASON TWO:

Corn Snake

"Little Boxes," Elvis Costello
"Bathtime in Clerkenwell," The Real
    Tuesday Weld
"Fuck Was I," Jenny Owen Youngs

Cooking with Jesus

"Little Boxes," Death Cab for Cutie
"Jammin Nation," Rocky Dawuni
"Rolling Stone from Texas," Don Walser
"Crazy Dazy," Chris Ligon
"Jah Be for Us," Rocky Dawuni

Last Tango in Agrestic

"Little Boxes," Engelbert Humperdinck
"Gamble Everything for Love," Ben Lee
"Strange Things Are Happening," Fern Jones
"Little Monkey," Gwendolyn

A.K.A. The Plant

"Little Boxes (Petites Boites)," McGarrigle Sisters
"Wraith Pinned to the Mist and OtherGames,"
    Of Montreal

Mrs. Botwin's Neighborhood

"Little Boxes," Maestro Charles Barnett
"Yodeling the Mozart," Mary Schneider
"Pirates," Gabby La La
"Love Thy Neighbor," Roaring Lion
"Kicking the Heart Out," Rogue Wave

Crush Girl Love Panic

"Little Boxes," Aidan Hawken
"Happy Clappy Birthday," Gwendolyn
"Od Lo Ahavti Dai," Yehoram Gaon
"Hadera," Alain Leroux

Must Find Toes

"Little Boxes," Ozomatli
"Let a Thug Smoke," The Individuals

MILF Money

"Little Boxes," The Submarines
"All Good," Zeroleen
"Vato," Snoop Dogg
"Not Enough," The 88
"Life Can Be Sunny," Roaring Lion

Bash

"Little Boxes," Tim DeLaughter of Polyphonic
    Spree
"Day on You," Tom Verlaine

Mile Deep and a Foot Wide

"Little Boxes," Regina Spektor
"Ghost of Corporate Future,"
    Regina Spektor
"Holland," Sufjan Stevens

Yeah. Like Tomatoes

"Little Boxes," Jenny Lewis
"You Look Like a Gorilla," The Mope

Pittsburgh

"Little Boxes," Malvina Reynolds
"One Thousand Tears of a Tarantula,"
    Dengue Fever
"Where Do We Go," Tracy Speuhler

ACKNOWLEDGMENTS

I felt incredibly lucky when I was given the opportunity to go behind the scenes and meet the extraordinary people who create *Weeds* and bring it to life on the small screen. From the moment I watched the pilot, I knew I was witnessing some of the finest American storytelling in any medium. Everybody with whom I spoke—on the cast and the crew—conveyed a rare, deep devotion to their work, and love and respect for the series and their colleagues, which is clearly conveyed in the scripts that I read, and the shows that we see.

The conversations I had with the writers, the cast, and the crew are some of the most engaging, hilarious, and memorable I've ever had. I am grateful to everyone who was able to speak with me, and impressed and touched by their generosity with their time, insights, and humor.

I'd especially like to thank Jenji Kohan, who is one of the most remarkable people I've ever encountered, virtually or otherwise. She's an übermensch, as warm and funny as she is brilliant. Mark Burley graciously and patiently gave me a lay of the land of *Weeds* and took on the herculean task of putting me in touch with the cast and crew during a time when the show was not in production. Roberto Benabib evoked the writers' room so vividly that it felt as exciting as being there. And I'd like to thank all of the publicists, managers, agents, and assistants who made the cast interviews—and, in turn, more than half of this book—possible.

Thank you to this awe-inspiring cast, who are as wonderful in person as they are on the stage and screen. What an honor it was to talk with Mary-Louise Parker, Elizabeth Perkins, Justin Kirk, Kevin Nealon, Tonye Patano, Romany Malco, Andy Milder, Hunter Parrish, Alexander Gould, Indigo, Allie Grant, Martin Donovan, Maulik Pancholy, Renée Victor, and Becky Thyre. Thank you, too, to the stellar stable of writers who spoke with me: Rolin Jones, Matthew Salsberg, Devon Shepard, and Shawn Schepps. And to the inventive, resourceful, very funny crew, who now know everything they ever (and possibly never) wanted to know about the marijuana "industry": Julie Bolder, Paul Boydston, Jode Mann, Amy McIntyre Britt,

Anya Colloff, David Helfand, Bill Turro, Gary Calamar, Gwendolyn Sanford, Brandon Young Jay, Amy Stofsky, and Craig Zisk.

Thank you, Lionsgate, for inviting me to do this project, and for all of their assistance: Kevin Beggs, Sandra Stern, and Andy Richley. At Showtime, thank you Bob Greenblatt and Danielle Gelber for talking *Weeds* with me, and for producing the most exciting series on television.

At Simon Spotlight Entertainment, my deep gratitude goes out to Terra Chalberg, Emily Westlake, and Tricia Boczkowski, and the production and art departments, for their smart editorial advice and enthusiasm for the project, and, not least of all, their tremendous patience.

Thank you to my agent and dear friend Lydia Wills at Paradigm, and her assistant, Jason Yarn. And a final word of gratitude to my spouse-equivalent-turned-part-time-transcriber, sounding board, and huge *Weeds* fan in her own right, Meredith Clair.

—Kera Bolonik

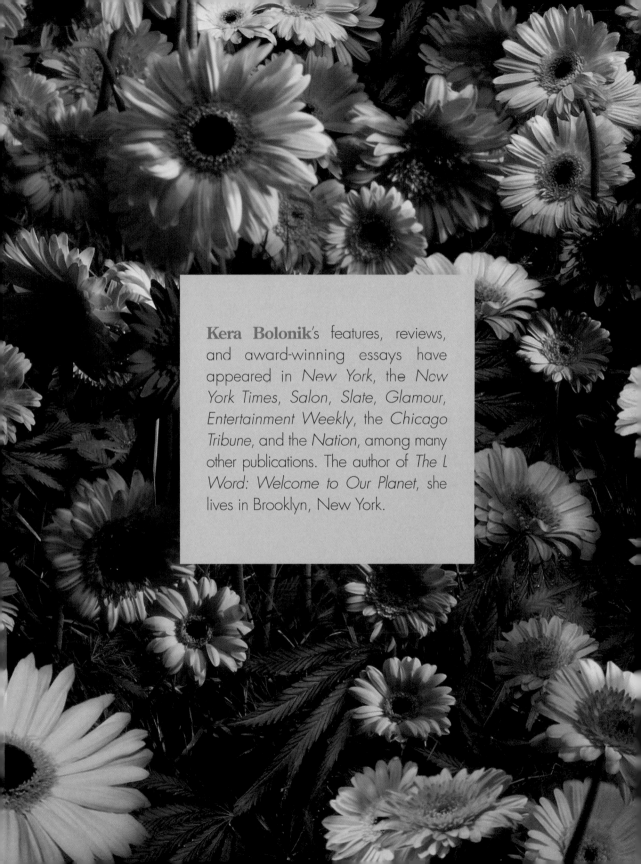

Kera Bolonik's features, reviews, and award-winning essays have appeared in *New York*, the *New York Times*, *Salon*, *Slate*, *Glamour*, *Entertainment Weekly*, the *Chicago Tribune*, and the *Nation*, among many other publications. The author of *The L Word: Welcome to Our Planet*, she lives in Brooklyn, New York.

GET WEEDS FOR YOUR OWN JOINT.

EACH DVD IS LOADED
WITH HIGH GRADE FEATURES

- Commentaries with Cast and Crew including
  Kevin Nealon, Romany Malco and others
- Showtime Original Content • Exclusive Featurettes • And Much More!

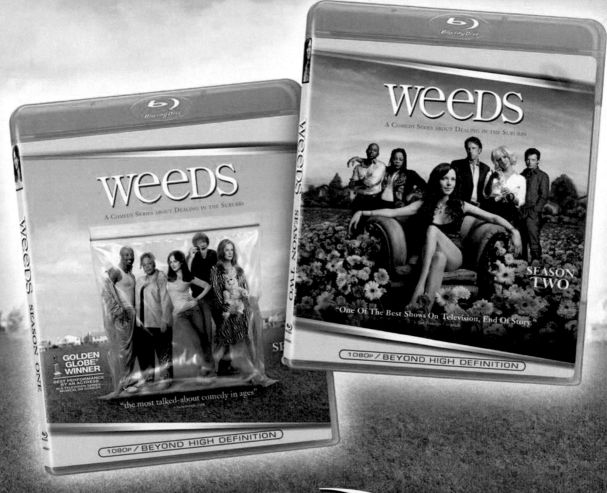